WRITING ANCHORS

*Explicit lessons that identify criteria,
offer strategic support,
and lead students to take ownership
of their writing*

JAN WELLS / JANINE REID

Pembroke Publishers Limited

© **2004 Pembroke Publishers**
538 Hood Road
Markham, Ontario, Canada L3R 3K9
www.pembrokepublishers.com

Distributed in the U.S. by Stenhouse Publishers
P.O. Box 11020
Portland, ME 04101

We acknowledge the financial support of the Government of Canada through the Book
Publishing Industry Development Program (BPIDP) for our publishing activities.

We acknowledge the Government of Ontario through the Ontario Media Development
Corporation's Ontario Book Initiative.

Library and Archives Canada Cataloguing in Publication

Wells, Jan, 1948-
     Writing anchors : explicit lessons that identify criteria, offer strategic support, and lead
students to take ownership of their writing / Jan Wells, Janine Reid.

ISBN 1-55138-180-X

1. English language—Composition and exercises—Study and teaching (Elementary)
2. Creative writing (Elementary education)
I. Reid, Janine, 1947- II. Title.

LB1576.W44 2004 372.62'3044   C2004-903972-5

Editor: Kate Revington
Cover Design: John Zehethofer
Cover Photo: Photo Disk
Typesetting: Jay Tee Graphics Ltd.

Printed and bound in Canada
9 8 7 6 5 4 3 2 1

Contents

Acknowledgments

At all stages in its development, *Writing Anchors* has been a collaborative effort. The primary teams in Vancouver Early Literacy Project Schools gave advice and added ideas. Colleagues in the Early Literacy Team were instrumental in shaping and refining the lessons. The ideas for the anchor lessons have been tried in classrooms and the notion of the skill focus for each lesson emerged from this classroom experience. As authors, we owe a debt of gratitude to all the teachers who have worked with us to shape the concept of *Writing Anchors*, but special thanks are due to Brenda Boylan, who developed the original workshops with us, Carollyne Sinclaire, who brought a special insight from her work with older students, the creative and dynamic Carrie Sleep, Janine's teaching partner, who supported the writing program in the classroom and contributed many original ideas, and Ulla Petersen, for her wisdom and insight into managing the Writing Workshop with young children. Thanks also to Carla Friesen, Jan Marsland, Dianna Mezzarobba, Noreen Morris and Joan Storlund for feedback, suggestions and student samples.

In acknowledging our thanks to those who have influenced us, we recognize that our work builds on the rich tradition of teaching writing that Donald Graves, Lucy McCormick Calkins, Shelley Harwayne, Nancie Atwell and David Booth have articulated. Their writing and teaching have been a cornerstone throughout our careers as teachers of young children. From them we have learned to open our hearts and minds to hear children's voices. The heartbeat of the Writing Workshop is the experience of the child, expressed in his or her words, and offered to us as a gift. Our role is to give children the tools to shape their words and craft their writing, allowing their voices to be heard.

Introduction: Unlocking Students' Personal Voice

Writing Anchors arises from our observations that teachers are looking for help with their writing programs. It is derived from a resource document called *Writers Alive!* that distilled ideas from a series of after-school workshops on writing. After a long day of teaching, teachers from the Vancouver School Board came together to share ideas, try new strategies and report back on their students' responses. The document developed over a two-year period.

Writing Anchors is based on the concept of anchor lessons. When we first introduced this concept to Vancouver teachers, we were overwhelmed by their enthusiastic response. Teachers learned how to help their students craft writing in four genres: personal recount, nonfiction, poetry and narrative. Time after time, they would tell us that they had lacked confidence in their ability to teach writing, but writing anchors gave them guidance and direction. Imagine our delight when, after a long workshop on a Friday afternoon, a teacher recklessly wished for her students to come back for the weekend "so I can teach them anchor lessons!"

For other teachers, daily journal writing has sufficed as the "writing program." When they ask students to write "a journal," however, they likely find that the writing is limited to a particular style. "Last night I ate spaghetti. Yesterday I played Nintendo." While journal writing has a place in every writing program, few of us lead lives of such variety and interest that they warrant daily reporting. We believe that journal writing alone does not make a writing program.

Many teachers report that they rely on Writing Workshop for regular practice in writing, but lack insight into how to teach writing craft explicitly in an authentic manner. These teachers want to help students unlock their personal voice. Anchor lessons are designed to help them do that.

Anchor lessons show students how to develop their writing more fully in all four major genres. With the anchor lessons, teachers learn how to guide their students towards a greater understanding of the craft of writing. An anchor lesson incorporates all the features of the traditional Writing Workshop, with pre-writing activities, mini-lessons, drafting, sharing with peers, conferencing with the teacher, revision and editing, followed, in some cases, by publishing and celebration. What distinguishes these anchor lessons is their place in a year-long writing program. Situated within a plan for the year, each anchor lesson focuses on a particular skill which can be integrated into future writing done in the Writing Workshop. The skill, or anchor, is introduced through mini-lessons, through pre-writing activities, through teacher read-alouds and in a whole host of ways that get the message across. The anchor becomes the focus of a sequence of activities leading to the completion of a polished piece of writing. It is a lesson to remember. It becomes part of the collective memory of the classroom community.

All the students participate in the anchor lesson, and the teacher participates at all stages of the lesson: coaching, monitoring, assessing progress and giving feedback. At the end of the anchor lesson, the class reflects on the learning that took place. They articulate the anchor and name it. The students write "Reflections on My Writing," using a journal or Blackline Master 1.1. A visual reminder is placed on a bulletin board, perhaps as a cue card, or is added to a student notebook or checklist. The students are encouraged to apply what they have learned in the anchor lesson in their independent writing.

Anchor lessons are threaded through the year. They should not dominate or be the whole program. Students need time to write on topics of their own choosing. They need to choose the genre and the style of their writing, as well as participate in teacher-led lessons. The writing anchors are a point of reference for teacher and students alike, reminding them of the skills that have been taught and providing a focus for conferences.

The skills, or anchors, are related to criteria that make expectations for fully developed writing explicit and attainable. The criteria are expressed in the Writing Profiles for personal writing, nonfiction, poetry and narrative writing. The Writing Profiles provide descriptions of writing in four dimensions: Engagement with the Topic, Vividness and Language Use, Organization and Structure, and Conventions. Students and teachers can use the Writing Profiles to assess a piece of writing. How well does the writing meet the descriptor? Does it meet the criteria?

When we make full use of the Writing Profiles and teach anchor lessons, we help students to become more aware of the skills they are using in their writing. They are encouraged to think about which skills they have applied, and where a particular skill would be effective in a piece of writing. This metacognitive awareness is one of the major goals of the anchor lessons. We want students to be more mindful of the techniques they are using, to select words with care and to be aware of the choices they can make as writers. To this end, we have built in a student reflection component both in discussion and writing at the end of each anchor lesson. The lessons provide scaffolding towards greater understanding of the craft of writing and thus raise the quality of students' independent writing.

How does this work in practice? "Zooming In on a Personal Moment" is one of the anchor lessons. It refers to the skill of expanding a moment in time, a technique which can be used not only in personal writing, but across the genres. After the lesson, students brainstorm ways in which the message of this anchor lesson could be represented visually. For example, a magnifying glass or a camera might suggest the idea of "coming in for a close-up look," which this lesson teaches. The class could represent this image on a cue card on a bulletin board. They could write a journal entry about zooming in and draw an image to represent the meaning they take from the lesson. A checklist could be placed at the back of a notebook or in a folder, and this anchor cue added. As the year progresses, the teacher will remind the class to "Zoom in" when appropriate in their writing. The anchor cues remind them of the repertoire of skills that they have developed and can draw on as they write.

One class that has worked with anchor lessons developed special bookmarks. As each anchor lesson was completed, the students designed a symbol or cue that would remind them of the learning from that lesson. They added the symbol to their bookmarks and used the bookmarks in their independent reading. On one side of the bookmark were the cues from the anchor lessons; on the other side, they wrote a list of pre-writing strategies that they had tried, for example: make a web, use a story map, sketch, cartoon, use a graphic organizer, and make a list.

Anchor lessons are grounded in the Writing Workshop. Their purpose is to enhance the work done in Writing Workshop, and they follow the Writing Workshop format. We have devoted Chapter 1 to our classroom practice in Writing Workshop, emphasizing the establishment of a supportive and predictable process, and the need to respond to students in developmentally

Zoom in!

appropriate ways that move the writing forward. Anchor lessons are not intended to put teachers up front and centre in Writing Workshop, but they *are* intended to show how skills can be taught and how the quality of student writing can be enhanced by a component of direct instruction.

The following diagram shows the relationship between a typical day in the Writing Workshop, where the writing is student directed, and an anchor lesson in which the teacher takes the lead.

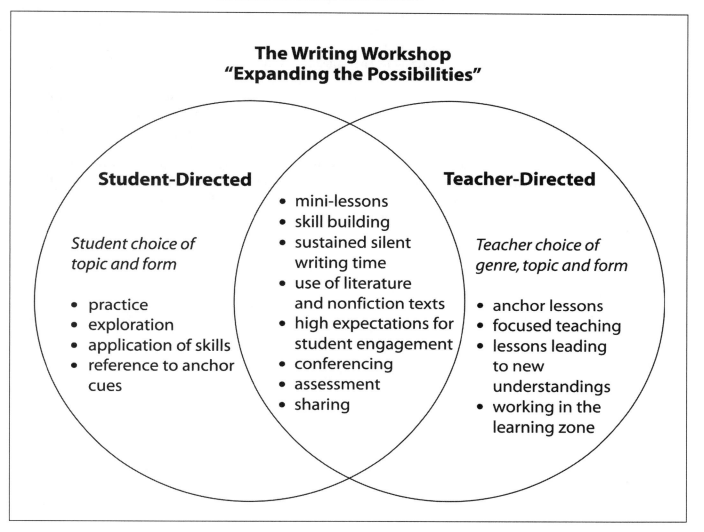

**The Writing Workshop
"Expanding the Possibilities"**

Student-Directed

Student choice of topic and form

- practice
- exploration
- application of skills
- reference to anchor cues

- mini-lessons
- skill building
- sustained silent writing time
- use of literature and nonfiction texts
- high expectations for student engagement
- conferencing
- assessment
- sharing

Teacher-Directed

Teacher choice of genre, topic and form

- anchor lessons
- focused teaching
- lessons leading to new understandings
- working in the learning zone

Writing Anchors is geared to students in Grades 2 to 7, who have a solid foundation in writing skills and are ready to experiment with personal, nonfiction, poetic and narrative forms of writing. These students use writing purposefully in all subjects across the curriculum. They are ready to craft their writing and experiment with new forms and styles of writing. Who are these students? What have we observed in writing classrooms? Let us introduce you to some of the students who inspired the lessons in *Writing Anchors*.

First, meet Carly. Carly reads fairy tales and writes long, involved tales of her own. She has a passion for writing, but seems to be lost in a morass of words. Her plots are convoluted with many undefined characters. Her teacher reads page after page of her work and wonders how best to help Carly craft her pieces succinctly.

Next, there's Jerry who has a passion for dolphins. He reads everything he can about the types and habits of dolphins. He writes nonfiction accounts from his reading, but he lacks understanding about the forms and conventions of nonfiction and how to craft his writing in this genre. His writing can be stilted and encyclopedic, lacking voice and structure.

Finally, meet Iman. He is a capable writer. Like most students his age, he is satisfied with his written products and responsive to limited revisions. He will add an ending or a new beginning or include a sentence that provides more detail. Iman will learn that, as he progresses through the grades, he will be asked to revise his work increasingly.

The writing teacher must find ways within this diversity of the Writing Workshop to respond to the complex needs of the class. *Writing Anchors* demonstrates how to support students through the structure of the Writing Workshop and how to assist them with explicit teaching of lessons on the craft of writing. Students' new understandings can be applied across the curriculum in science, social studies, math and all the academic areas. Writing in different genres feeds the students' interests and imaginations in the Writing Workshop.

We believe that the teacher has an active role to play in a balanced writing program. *Writing Anchors* provides both the teacher and the students with a road map for the writing journey.

1

The Writing Workshop: Establishing Ritual, Routine and Rejoicing

Writing Workshop is the cornerstone of our program. It happens daily, as much as possible. It lasts for at least an hour, longer if it can. It is a routine, regular and prized by the students. They look forward to it and become familiar with its structures and routines.

As teachers, we are guided by two beliefs about our role in Writing Workshop. We believe that we must create a supportive classroom environment that encourages risk taking. We also believe that we need to understand the craft of writing and the skills that our students need to learn. We must be knowledgeable about writing.

Creating a supportive environment is one key to the success of Writing Workshop. When we achieve this, we engage the imagination of the learner and encourage risk taking and self-expression. The climate of the classroom, both emotional and physical, contributes to the students' willingness and eagerness to write. Good classroom management that places high expectations on students contributes to the climate. We need to be organized with materials ready and available. Routines for getting started, moving from place to place in the room, finding a partner and putting work away at the end of the workshop are all part of the things we have to consider.

The supportive classroom also acknowledges effort and achievement. We celebrate students' personal bests. We rejoice in the successes and we use student examples to illustrate ideas. We have an Author's Chair and a place for students to read one another's writing. We teach appropriate ways for students to respond to one another and we model ways of responding. We publish student writing in books and let students borrow them for home reading. These and many other rituals and routines contribute to the establishment of a classroom where a "can do" spirit is evident. Many students come to school convinced that they have nothing to say. We show them the importance of reading and writing in our own lives and take them on the journey with us.

Building a "Can Do" Spirit

Here are some of the rituals and routines that have helped us build the "can do" spirit in our classrooms.

Provide a daily writing time.

Frequent opportunities to write combined with appropriate teaching equals dramatic growth. We strive to provide a daily writing time at all grade levels.

The Writing Worshop

Publishing*

- the making of a good copy
- enhanced by illustration
- shared as a reading to an audience

Before Students Write

Warm up the writers with rich experiences, e.g.,
- read-alouds
- partner talk
- mini-lessons

Planning the Writing

Encourage use of tools for shaping the writing:
- webs
- lists
- drawings
- notes

Teacher Conference

- response
- further revision and editing
- reflection on the process
- setting of goals

The Writing Process

Drafting

- a concentrated focus on ideas and language
- conventions applied with the best effort possible (spelling, punctuation, legibility)
- a usually silent process
- self-editing and revising with an eraser

Peer Conference

- reading to a friend
- adding or taking away
- fixing the meaning
- fixing the spelling and punctuation

* Not all pieces of writing are published.

Read aloud every day—writers need to read and be read to.

By hearing stories read and responding to them, students develop an appreciation for rich language and vivid expression, the elements of story, and the wide range of forms available for writing. Hearing the work of exemplary children's authors, their teachers, and their classmates inspires students to play in the world of words.

Teachers must make a heightened awareness of vocabulary and an appreciation of the gift of words deliberate in discussions about read-alouds. In writing-rich classrooms, students are given opportunities to develop lists of images and rich language that excite the imagination of the class. Students can draw on these references and expand their understanding of well-chosen language.

After reading aloud, the conversation may be about character traits, the problems encountered in stories, and alternative solutions. Good beginnings that hook the reader and fine conclusions that end a piece in a satisfying manner are found and discussed. Over time, the writer's craft, the emotion and energy conveyed in well-chosen texts, and the discussions about these texts do much to strengthen students' writing. In addition, a text read aloud may be the hook that starts an anchor lesson.

Great writers need to hear great writing. Choose your read-alouds carefully to illustrate aspects of powerful writing. Examples of good books to use are listed at the back of this book.

Provide regular pre-writing activities—writers need to warm up and rehearse their ideas.

Warming up the writers has two important functions. First, it gets the juices flowing. It builds anticipation for the writing to come and generates a sense of excitement in the classroom. Second, the warm-up activities help to push the expectations, moving the writing to increasing levels of expressiveness of language and competence with conventions. Here are some powerful ways to do this.

Use oral rehearsals: If they can't say it, they can't write it. Picture-making is appropriate for non-fluent writers, but most students in later grades do not need to draw a picture to rehearse their ideas for writing. By this time they have become relatively fluent, and their ability to write has surpassed their ability to communicate through drawing. The challenge at this age is to make their writing catch up to their talking.

To facilitate talking as rehearsal, young students are seated "knee to knee and eye to eye" with another person. They decide who is A and who is B. Older students can simply turn to a partner nearby.

Throughout the lesson, ask students to turn to their partners and respond according to teacher directions. If the lesson is on retelling a story, for example, the teacher stops frequently while reading aloud and asks students to retell sections of the story to their partners. These talks can help students attain the individuality that becomes the "writer's voice."

Partner talk as a precursor to writing is useful in Writing Workshop and in the anchor lessons.

Carrie Sleep, a skilled Vancouver teacher, has engineered four sets of color-coded partnerships for the students in her class. She refers to the colors to expedite forming partners. She simply says to the class, "I want you to meet with your blue partner for this activity today."

Use drama: Warming up the writing can be achieved very effectively using a wide range of drama techniques. Larry Swartz, in *The New Dramathemes*, describes techniques that engage students in role play, interviewing, and seeing ideas and issues from multiple perspectives. Doing these activities before writing can give the student greater control of a topic and enrich the writer's personal voice. Several of our anchor lesson plans use drama techniques to warm up the writing.

Celebrate writing from the previous day to warm up ideas for today: Take time at the beginning of every Writing Workshop to showcase student growth. Rejoice in the successes and show how everyone can learn from their classmates. In this way, all students are recognized for their incremental effort and improvement, and others are inspired by new ideas. In these sessions, the teacher selects passages to read aloud or chooses a student to sit in the Author's Chair to read his or her work aloud. Here is a sampling of constructive comments that might further student thought and discussion.

- "Listen to the exciting lead in Paivand's story."
- "What makes Jaswinder's closing effective?"
- "Listen to the 'gems' in Fariba's writing today."
- "Chris started in the middle of the action. Why do you think that might be effective?"
- "Your use of transition words really helps pace the story."
- "I love the imagery you are using here. Well done!"
- "What did you find powerful in this piece?"

In *Writing Anchors* we have included many writing samples from students we have taught. Many pieces come from Janine's Grade 3 classroom. We hope teachers may make use of these samples to show their students what young writers can do. We believe that these samples can inspire students at any grade level as the skills demonstrated are a matter of degree, not of substance. Samples of student writing can be photocopied and shared on an overhead. Students may be given a copy of a student sample, and individually or in pairs, they may critique what makes this writing special. They might suggest ways to improve the piece or add to its impact.

It remains our steadfast belief that the best examples for explicit teaching come from writing done by students. We observe that students will strive to emulate successful models in the class. Effective writing teachers provide opportunities to share and celebrate breakthroughs or "personal bests," such as you can see above, with the class. When teachers select writing to celebrate at the beginning of each Writing Workshop, they must look for trends, asking themselves, "How can I use this piece of writing to advance the understanding of the class? What can this student do that others need to learn?" Put student samples on overheads and discuss them with the class. "What's missing? What's powerful? Why have I chosen this? What makes this a good piece?"

Writers need to own their topics.

Students need time to experiment with their own ideas. Free choice of topics can lead to productive writing and teachers need to provide time for students to write stories, poems, personal accounts and informational texts on topics of their own choosing. It is the student's job to think of a writing topic in the regular course of the Writing Workshop. We suggest to our students that they should let their brains consider ideas for writing when they put their heads on the pillow at night. It is their homework to have a writing idea.

Students may need a conference occasionally to get them going. It may be helpful for the teacher to adopt one of the following approaches.

- Say something like the following: "Having trouble getting started? Let's talk a minute about what you might like to write about. What do you enjoy? Let's start a web together to capture some of your ideas. Then you can zoom in on your favorite section when you've had time to think."
- Refer to stories read aloud or shared by other students: "Can you remember a time you experienced something like that? What was that like for you?"
- Suggest that students modify a familiar story.
- Remind students of forms or topics the class is studying.

At the end of a day, with a cup of tea and a pile of writing books at hand, we are delighted to review the variety of topics and forms that emerge from the Writing Workshop. From nonfiction accounts about wolves to poems for a friend's birthday, the Writing Workshop echoes the cadence of student passions.

Writers need silence.

The Writing Workshop is a quiet, purposeful time. Students must be given ample time to warm up their ideas orally prior to writing. They may be mumble-reading their passages aloud, but there will be no chatty conversations among them. (Mumble-reading is *sotto voce* reading to oneself to hear the sounds of the words.) When we gave this message at a workshop, one skeptical teacher reported: "I tried silence. What a difference it made in the writing!" Students who work on their writing in focused, quiet environments show the greatest gains.

Writers need a risk-free environment.

Many students and some teachers want the reassurance of "correctness" at the expense of self-expression, particularly when students have been taught at home to seek perfection. One of the biggest risks for students is to write fearlessly and expressively without being overly concerned with spelling perfection. It is the teacher's art to create an atmosphere where risk taking and expressiveness have value equal to correctness.

With this understanding in mind, use writing dictionaries, word lists and word walls with caution. They can become convenient writing avoidance mechanisms for reluctant writers. They can impede writing fluency as students stop frequently to look up a word rather than continue to write their best approximations. Over-reliance on spelling aids can create an expectation that perfection is more important than risk taking, fluency and expressiveness.

Teachers can help students overcome these fears by celebrating risk taking. This is not to say that "anything goes." We suggest that before students submit their work, they check their spelling and underline spelling approximations for which they wish to learn standard spellings. We recommend that students use spelling references in the class during the last 10 minutes of Writing Workshop to look up words. We also hold students accountable for spelling words that have been taught or are in view in the room. Older students are encouraged to revise their first drafts for clarity of meaning after they have mumble-read and before conferencing with peers or their teachers.

In our experience, some students use perfect penmanship as a means of writing avoidance. They repeatedly erase and rewrite, apparently trying to get the perfect letter formation rather than having the confidence to write freely. In regards to penmanship, we encourage younger students to write legibly from the start because they seldom revise and publish; however, perfect printing or writing is not the main objective. Once again, it is the teacher's art to find the balance between creating a risk-free environment and setting high expectations.

For students in Grades 2 and 3, we suggest that teachers seldom require "published work" — that is, work that has been finely edited and recopied. Publishing takes time away from crafting new pieces of writing and should be restricted to short pieces once or twice per term. Students in Grades 4 to 7 are more adept at revising and editing their work and may publish work more often. There needs to be, however, an expectation that students will compose their first drafts with care and that they will write neatly and legibly — even in the Writing Workshop.

Writers need high expectations for effort and application.

We expect students to apply themselves with diligence to writing for extended periods of time. Our belief is that students will sustain their writing efforts when they are supported with warm-up activities, modelling, criteria, and celebration. In addition, we are constantly working the room as students are writing. We take a chair around so that we can stop to talk briefly with each student at eye level. One of the purposes of this encounter is to encourage and affirm each writer's efforts. Helpful comments might sound like the following:

- "I like your title. It really catches my attention."
- "I see you rereading what you have written. That's something good writers do."
- "That's a great lead you've used."

We also look for opportunities to extend the writing, particularly for "fast finishers." When we sit with the fast finishers and discuss the writing with prompts and questions, they can always see a place to extend their work. We encourage students to write for the whole time.

Encourage the class to write as much as they can in the time allotted. Gently nudge them towards increasing volume. Provide graphic organizers to help students stay focused on a topic. Establish clear criteria for the product so the student can revisit the work. Encourage students to use first drafts corrected throughout the year as pieces to revise and strengthen. Provide opportunities for students to do "quick-writes" (10–15 minutes) to develop fluency. Suggest retelling a familiar story as a bridge for students experiencing output problems.

As we circulate, we are on the lookout for images and phrases that are particularly well crafted. In September and October, we stop the writers and direct their attention to these powerful examples of rich language used in the class. We might say, "Stop everyone and listen to the way Jessica has started her writing today," or "Listen to the way Mindy describes the breakfast she ate today." In this way the writers are encouraged and challenged to stretch themselves to seek out gems in their own writing. They also hear good models and get ideas from peers.

Later in the year, as students gain confidence in writing, it is unnecessary to interrupt the flow of their ideas by commenting on writing gems during writing. Save these conversations for sharing times. This helps to keep students focused on the writing task.

As students' confidence increases over time, so do teachers' expectations for effort, volume, and levels of convention use and expressiveness. When the teacher moves in the classroom supporting students with gentle suggestions and encouragement, students' confidence increases and they redouble their efforts to write well.

Writers need to know adults as authors.

It is a powerful lesson when teachers share the drafts of letters, notices, poems, or stories that they are working on themselves. When we take the risk to share our writing, we become one in a community of writers. We model the struggles of authoring for our students, showing them how drafting and revising can improve a piece of work. Some teachers take the time to draft their own pieces while the students are working. Others bring into class an example of something they have written. (In the poetry anchor lessons you will find a poem that was written by Janine in the Writing Workshop. Writing by teachers, shared with the class as an example of a way to respond to an idea, generates great interest and discussion among the class.)

Another way to show students the importance of writing in our lives is to invite an author into the classroom. Your teacher-librarian can help arrange author visits for several classes at a time. The experience of meeting a real live author and talking about the writing process is stimulating for students and leads to a renewed enthusiasm for reading and writing. Authors will often emphasize the importance of revising, making careful observations and keeping notebooks full of jottings and ideas that might develop into fully fledged pieces.

A Typical Day in the Writing Workshop

Let's look in on a typical day in the Writing Workshop. As you read, note how the students are supported by the predictability of the workshop. Note, too, the type of support the teacher offers as she circulates to meet with the writers at work.

February 13, Grade 2: The children have Valentine's Day on their minds. They have been doing shared reading with Valentine poems and making cards for friends and family.

Teacher	Students	Purpose
"*I want to show you some writing done by your classmates in the Writing Workshop yesterday. Listen to these and see if you can tell why I have chosen them.*" Teacher or student reads aloud examples of great story language, a good beginning and/or ending sentence, a novel choice of topic or format, a personal best.	• Listen • Participate by reading samples	• Celebrating • Modelling
The teacher reads aloud *Rosie and Michael* by Judith Viorst as an example of expressive writing on the theme of friendship, and says, "*You may want to write about your feelings of love or friendship for someone that you know today or not. The choice is yours.*"	• Listen	• Demonstrating ideas and examples of expressive language • Focusing
"*You have another choice to make today. You may choose the form of writing too. Let's list all the ways you know how to write: story, letter, poem, journal, nonfiction, cartoon, list, newspaper article, writing in role, writing from another point of view, making a comic strip, making a computer slide show. Stop and think for a moment of two things: first, the form your writing will take today, and second, the subject of your writing. Put up one finger when you know the form and another finger when you know the subject. Like this: 'I will write a poem about a penguin,' or 'I will write a journal about my birthday this week.'*"	• Put up fingers to indicate choice	• Deciding on a form • Giving students choice and ownership
"*Turn to a partner and tell them what you will be writing about today.*"	• Converse • Share ideas	• Making a plan
"*When you go back to your seat, start with your thinking page. You need to get some juicy ideas for your writing. You can make a web, a sketch, a list of juicy words, or some phrases you want to include. I will give you 10 minutes to plan your writing for today.*"	• Make web, sketch, or list	• Planning • Focusing • Developing vocabulary
Teacher circulates, stopping to confer with individual students who are having difficulty. Students are encouraged to write "for the whole writing time."	• Write	• Providing quiet, focused time for writing with teacher's support
Teacher facilitates partner response: students meet partners on the floor to share their stories. They respond to their partner with "two stars and a wish" and move on to read and listen again to another partner.	• Read their work to their partners	• Clarifying • Sharing ideas • Celebrating

Teacher	Students	Purpose
Teacher facilitates a group share: When the teacher has met most of the students to scan the writing and given each one a nudge or a compliment, she calls the group together as a whole for a debrief. She says, "*Turn to a partner near you on the carpet and tell them what form you chose to write in today. Also, tell your partner what topic you chose for your writing. Tell your partner what you enjoyed about your writing today.*" The teacher then chooses a student to sit in the "Author's Chair" and read his/her work aloud. The Writing Workshop ends with applause.	• Author's Chair	• Celebrating

The most important thing I can suggest is that we do not abbreviate the Writing Workshop so that it lasts only as long as our children's attention for writing lasts. One of our major goals at this point is to encourage children to say more, to sustain their work longer, to approach a text expecting it to be more detailed and all of this means that we need to give children more time for writing than they know what to do with.

Lucy Calkins, *The Art of Teaching Writing*, p. 115

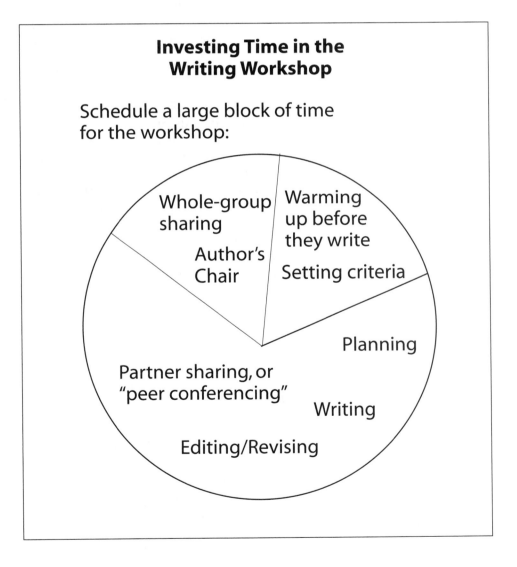

Investing Time in the Writing Workshop

Schedule a large block of time for the workshop:

- Whole-group sharing
- Author's Chair
- Warming up before they write
- Setting criteria
- Planning
- Writing
- Editing/Revising
- Partner sharing, or "peer conferencing"

Examples of conferences with students who are having difficulty

Conferencing before writing: Here are two exchanges between the teacher and individual students. Ming is a new English-speaker.

TEACHER: What will you write today?

MING: A story about a dragon.

TEACHER: Tell me about your dragon.

MING: He lives in a castle.

TEACHER: What is the problem?

MING: Man coming. Bad man.

TEACHER: What does he want?

MING: Castle.

TEACHER: What will happen?

MING: Dragon will . . .

TEACHER: Blow fire on him?

MING: Yes.

TEACHER: Are you ready to write?

MING: Yes.

> Feb 13 2003
> My story   Ming
> One day a dragon lived
> in a castle. The castle is
> dragon's home. One day
> he saw a man, the man
> said "Ha! Ha! I will brocken
> your castle." and he did.
> The dragon is mad and
> make fire the man...

Ophelia has written "Poem For Mom and dad About Valentine's Day," but she is stuck.

TEACHER: Let's write down some of the things that make your mom special to you.

Ophelia and teacher develop a list together.

TEACHER: Now you do the same kind of list for your dad and I will come back to see you.

When the teacher returns, she works with Ophelia to change "places" to "Toys R Us," "stuff" to "pizza," and "things" to "bird houses," and sets Ophelia to work to shape her poem with her new notes.

> Poem   Ophelia
> For Mom + dad
> About Valentines Day
>
> | Mom | Dad |
> |-----|-----|
> | | ✓ helps me with Math |
> | ✓ help me with | ✓ Takes me to Toys Я Us |
> | ✓ home work | ✓ Makes pizza |
> | room | Makes bird houses for me |
> | tucks me in | ✓ Does hair dow |
> | reads a story | ✓ Makes my Birthday cards |
> | ✓ egg sandwich | · Buys shoes for me |

18

Conferencing during writing: As Kim is developing her thinking page, the teacher notices that it has potential as a poem and encourages her to develop the list into a poem form. "You've really got some great ideas in your poem, Kim. Let's work together to make your poem follow a pattern that will please the reader."

```
Feb 13, 2003          Why?
    I wonder why hens could lay eggs
why Authors get good in imaginacion
why a camel has bumps
why tears are salty
    Why God has powers
    Why clocks can tell time
why cats have whiskers
why shooting stars give wishes
why Jerry likes dolphins
why Ashley likes tap danceing
    How people make sparkles
Why when spring and summer comes And
    fill my house
Why chacklits taste good
why robins have wings
    I think thats all I wonder about
but maybe more tomorrow.
```

When the Writing Workshop is part of daily practice from Kindergarten through the grades, students understand that their role is to bring ideas and motivation to the task of writing. When we honor what they bring and give them opportunities to express their writer's voice in the forms of their choosing, we gain insight into the mind and experience of the child. Provided with daily writing time, plenty of encouragement and celebration, rich examples and gentle nudges, students will thrive as writers.

The chart on the next page reflects what students at different developmental stages can do as writers.

Developing Expectations for the Writing Workshop from Kindergarten to Grade 7

Emergent/Beginning Writers (Kindergarten to Grade 1)	Consolidating and Fluent Writers (Grades 2–3)	Fluent Writers (Grades 4–7)
• rehearse with pictures, talk or webs • own the topic • not yet ready to revise, but may be nudged to add • use "invented spelling" • publish rarely	• rehearse with talk, webs, and drawing • can do limited revision mostly in terms of adding details, changing occasional words, adding endings or beginnings • can check own and a partner's work for spelling and punctuation • may attempt paragraphing • can work towards anchor lesson criteria • can apply anchor lessons to Writing Workshop with guidance • can work in varied forms • publish occasionally • keep a portfolio with help	• rehearse with webs, maps, drafts, lists, and so on • self-edit — apply known spelling, grammar, and punctuation • peer-edit • apply anchor lessons to Writing Workshop with increasing independence • understand anchor lesson criteria and self-evaluate using them • able to work towards substantial revisions at the level of the word, the sentence, the paragraph and the whole • able to work towards substantial revisions of writing through reorganizing, deleting, inserting, extending and crafting the writing to better match criteria • work towards publishing regularly • keep a portfolio

Working in the Learning Zone

So far we have discussed how teachers establish rituals, routines and celebrations of student writing to create a risk-free environment and a "can do" spirit in Writing Workshop.

The second important contribution that teachers make to student learning is the knowledge we bring about the craft of writing and how we apply it. To help students develop their skills and refine their work, we work gently in the learning zone, the *zone of proximal development* as Vygotsky termed it, where learning can take place.

In the learning zone, students are ready to take on the next concept. The teacher presents a challenge that is neither too easy nor too difficult. Working in the zone is demanding for teachers. It requires a thorough knowledge of student development and careful observation of individuals as they work in the classroom. In the Writing Workshop, we sometimes push and sometimes hold back, depending on our knowledge of the student. Our judgment is informed by careful observations and assessment of students and their writing using the Writing Profiles. The Writing Profiles give us insights into what we need to teach and our students' needs as writers.

Teachers who become knowledgeable about the craft of writing are able to make helpful suggestions and read student work critically in the best sense of the adverb. They know how to seize the teachable moment and make connections to previous learning. With the anchor lessons in place, they can refer back to the ones that have been taught or look ahead to which one would be best to teach next depending on class needs. They can hold specific and focused conferences with young writers, responding to the writing with reference to the skills that the students have learned.

Working in the learning zone requires that teachers

- become knowledgeable about the craft of writing
- respond to what students write
- provide specific instruction in the craft of writing

Each of these elements is discussed below.

Become knowledgeable about the craft of writing.

Writing teachers need to engage in writing and understand the craft of writing. Assessment tools provide a wonderful starting place for teachers wanting to deepen their understanding of the writing craft. The criteria by which we judge a piece of writing give us guidance in crafting our lessons and conferences. In *Writing Anchors*, we present Writing Profiles organized around four dimensions of writing: Engagement with the Topic, Vividness and Language Use, Organization and Structure, and Conventions. **As students mature and develop as writers, we believe that their writing demonstrates a difference of *degree* in each dimension, but *not* of substance.** All grades need instruction in all four aspects. The assessment of performance on these dimensions will depend upon the teachers' understanding of how much students at different ages can be expected to do and in how much detail. However, the descriptors from grade to grade are identical. Let's take a look at each aspect in turn.

Engagement with the Topic refers first to the meaning, ideas and details the writer includes about the topic. Is the topic focused? Are ideas clearly expressed and understandable? Is the purpose of the writing clear? Is the writing easy to follow with relevant and logical ideas about the topic?

Second, Engagement with the Topic refers to detail and elaboration of ideas. Are details relevant? Are the ideas supported by specific, relevant examples? Is there elaboration of ideas through engaging details such as explanations, examples, opinions, feelings, and comparisons?

Dimension: Engagement with the Topic

Strong Writing	*Weaker Writing*
• is focused and easy to read • has fully developed ideas supported by relevant details • creates an impact	• is unclear or illogical • has few ideas or ideas that are vague and unsupported by detail • is brief

Vividness and Language Use includes ideas about energy, passion, voice, word choice, expressiveness, variety, originality and creativity. There is an element of experimentation and risk taking in this dimension. Being precise, finding the right word to do the job, varying sentence length and pattern, and using language to create special effects are all part of this dimension.

In assessing the work, teachers must consider if the voice of the writer is clearly heard in the piece. Is there energy, originality and insight in the writing? Does the writer's personal perspective come through? If a piece is vivid, it is unique to the individual and, when read aloud, has a wide audience appeal. These elements work together in this dimension to create the writer's "voice," or unique personality.

Dimension: Vividness and Language Use

Strong Writing	*Weaker Writing*
• shows a high degree of individual expression, passion and energy for the topic, and the writer's unique voice • includes words chosen for effect and possibly experimentation with poetic devices and sensory language • demonstrates risk taking with language and sentence structure • possesses a wider audience appeal	• relies on stereotypes or clichés • lacks passion and energy for the topic • relies on generic expression • employs simple language • lacks originality • has little appeal for a wider audience

Organization and Structure describes the rules and conventions of the form of writing. Organization and Structure is also about finding the right tone, text features and appropriate language for the content. A report is expressed differently from a friendly letter; a poem is not the same as a science experiment. Organization and Structure describes the way in which the writing follows the rules of the genre.

Organization and Structure also includes ideas about the organization of the writing, such as ideas about sequence, cohesion and completeness, length, headings, beginnings, conclusions and transitions.

Dimension: Organization and Structure

Strong Writing	*Weaker Writing*
• is logically sequenced • has smooth transitions marked by a variety of connecting words • includes a beginning, a middle and a conclusion • is cohesive and easy to follow	• may be brief with little or no introduction • links ideas with basic connecting words • may introduce a topic but lack a conclusion • loses focus and may be difficult to follow

Conventions refers to the surface features or mechanics of writing. It includes grammar, punctuation, spelling, and legibility. It is our expectation that by Grade 3, the writing of most students will contain minor errors in basic spelling, punctuation, and sentence structure, but these will not interfere with meaning. High-frequency words will be spelled correctly and "invented spelling" used only for unusual or unfamiliar words.

Dimension: Conventions

Strong Writing	*Weaker Writing*
• has few errors and these do not interfere with meaning • is legible and shows care	• is inconsistent in spelling, punctuation, grammar and legibility • contains errors that make the writing difficult to understand

Once teachers have internalized the descriptors of the dimensions of writing we are able to plan lessons that move the writing forward in each of these dimensions. We also know how to respond to student work in ways that are helpful in advancing students' understanding of a dimension.

Respond to what students write.

When teachers respond to students' writing they need to have a learning plan in mind for each student. The Writing Profiles that you will find in Chapters 2 to 5 will help you to select a focus for the conference. Knowing how to respond to students' writing is a skill that teachers develop with experience. It is a delicate balancing act between encouraging and motivating the student, and giving critical feedback. We believe that the teacher's insight in selecting an aspect of the writing to critique nudges the learner forward. Each conference is a teachable moment.

When we meet a student to conference about their writing, we ask ourselves, "What is the *one thing* that would be most helpful for this student at this time?" The answer to this question is contained in our understanding of the history of the student as a writer, the lessons that have been taught, the criteria for the piece of work and the stages of writing development.

With these things in mind, we choose one of the following types of responses to advance the writing:

Respond to engagement with the topic.

- "I saw you checking your work against the criteria for poetry. Are you satisfied that you have met the criteria? Which criteria do you think your writing best exemplifies?"
- "I like the way you have shown what this character looks like. You told the 'outside story.' Consider how you would add the 'inside story' to make your piece more powerful."
- "You've told the reader some of what happened. I'd like to know more about what it was like. How can you include sensory details so that the reader *lives* the experience too? What did it look like? feel like? sound like?"
- "Listen to what you said here. Does that make sense? Can you fix it so that it makes sense?"
- "I would like you to write some more today. Let's talk about what will happen next in your story."

Teachers can use the Writing Profiles with a highlighter pen to indicate student achievement in the dimensions. If the teacher changes pen color each term, but uses the same profile for each student, student progress is readily apparent as the colors change with student growth.

Teachers at A. R. Lord School in Vancouver met in grade groups and assessed student writing. For each grade level they chose samples of writing that exemplified their expectations for the genre at that grade. These writing samples were copied and put into binders for teachers to use as a reference when determining students' writing development and needs.

Some schools administer a writing task three times a year. This writing is then scored by teachers in grade groups and a school profile is developed. The writing samples are then placed in each student's portfolio, together with the Writing Profiles. The advantages of this school-wide process are in setting goals for the school as a whole, in developing a community of knowledgeable writing teachers, and in creating consistency of instruction and the language of instruction from grade to grade.

Respond to vividness, organization, and language use.

- "You have given a rich description here. Think about it with poet's eyes and see if you can create an image for your setting."
- "You have *told* us that you were happy. Can you think of a way to *show* us instead?"
- "This story is very satisfying. May I make one suggestion? I'd like you to look at your *said* words. Could you use the thesaurus for a wider variety of choices?"
- "This story is rich with ideas. When you highlighted the first word of every sentence, did you notice most sentences start the same way?"
- "In this section you talked about your time on the farm. You come back to it later in this part here. How can you sequence your work so that it flows more smoothly?"

Respond to conventions.

- "Do you remember we studied that word in spelling? Please fix it in this story."

Provide explicit instruction in the craft of writing.

Look for trends and seize the teachable moment: One of the most effective ways teachers can address the writing needs of their students is to look for trends while circulating in the Writing Workshop. For example, if you notice that many of the writing pieces end abruptly, call all the students for an impromptu mini-lesson on closing sentences. Tell them that closing sentences give the reader a signal and a sense of satisfaction that the piece is finished. If you have already taught the anchor lesson "Rebus Story: The Night I Followed the Dog," from Chapter 5, then you can refer back to that experience. Look at the writing anchor about ending your writing with a strong conclusion that you developed in that lesson. Remind the class of the anchor and ask students to revise their endings accordingly. If you have not taught this lesson yet, plan to introduce it in the near future so that everyone can develop a greater understanding of different ways to end a piece of writing with a "big finish."

Plan for growth — teach anchor lessons: The following chapters contain the anchor lessons we have developed in four forms: personal writing, nonfiction, poetry, and narrative writing. The anchor lessons illuminate the aspects of powerful writing in each of the forms through teacher modelling, demonstration, guided practice for the students and reflective activities that name the learning. Each anchor lesson follows the format of the daily Writing Workshop with pre-writing activities, drafting, editing and revising, conferencing, and sharing followed by reflection. Our experience has been that students who participate in carefully structured anchor lessons are able to apply what they have learned across the four genres in their independent writing. They can refer back to the writing anchors and remember the skills that have been learned. They soon understand that techniques used in one form can be applied in another. For example, as students learn "Poet's Eyes," the technique for developing metaphor and simile developed in anchor lessons in Chapter 4, they realize that this technique has application in personal recounts as well. In this way, new layers of understanding are created and skills overlap.

To extend student understanding, ask them to search for effective conclusions in their reading. They can record particularly effective examples and share them with one another. Perhaps they will begin to note different styles of conclusions and be able to categorize them.

The Potential of Anchor Lessons

The goal is to provide a toolbox of techniques for students to draw upon in their daily writing. The result of teaching anchor lessons is the creation of a classroom culture and language with which to talk about writing. The side-effects of the anchor lessons can be felt in all subjects across the curriculum as students use their writing anchors to describe the skills they are using.

How often do we teach anchor lessons? One or two from each of the four forms might be introduced each term, giving students a basis upon which to build their repertoire for Writing Workshop. Schools where all the teachers have a Writing Workshop focus find that students are keen to write and ready to learn new techniques. By and large, students enjoy having the form of the writing chosen for them, and when topic and form are set, they can concentrate on language choice and technique rather than on searching for ideas.

Some teachers like to teach units based on genres. A story unit, for example, might take six to eight weeks. Three or four of the anchor lessons from the narrative writing section might be chosen before students are asked to write an original story at the conclusion of the unit. No one should plan to do all the anchor lessons in a genre. Rather, choose selectively the ones that appeal to you the most and meet the needs of your students.

We imagine teachers taking the anchor lessons and changing them to fit their own style and the needs of their students. We see teachers refining the lessons, adding to them and editing them to suit. We see teachers creating new anchor lessons of their own and sharing ideas with other staff members. One thing is clear: when a school creates a culture of writing and all the students see themselves and their teachers as writers, then the possibilities are endless. We hope these anchor lessons will provide you with experiences for your students that will lead to successful, powerful writing and generate an excitement about writing in your classroom and beyond.

Reflections on My Writing

Name: _____   Date: _____

My Title _____

Form (recount, nonfiction, poetry, narrative) _____

1. What did I learn about writing from this lesson?

2. What steps did we follow?

3. How did this lesson help me?

4. How will I use what I've learned in my writing from now on?

5. What is my next writing goal?

2

Writing Personal Recounts

Anchor Lesson	Skill Focus
Zooming In on a Personal Moment	Zooming in on a moment; telling the inside and outside stories; using dialogue to add impact; telling details only the writer knows
Scaffolding Recount with Smooth Transitions	Using transitional words appropriately
The Friday Journal: A Personal Account with Details	Zooming in on a moment; telling the inside and outside stories; using dialogue to add impact; telling details only the writer knows
Collections: Adding Detail from Personal Experience	Zooming in on a moment; telling the inside and outside stories; using dialogue to add impact; telling details only the writer knows
Show, Don't Tell: My Teacher	Removing adjectives and demonstrating by examples
Special Places	Zooming in on a moment; telling the inside and outside stories; using dialogue to add impact; telling details only the writer knows
Find a Hook	Starting with a great lead
Recounting or Retelling a Story	Synthesizing and summarizing information
The Gift of Words	Developing vocabulary
Connecting	Connecting literature to personal experience
Reflecting and Evaluating	Expressing personal opinions

Personal writing is the form that teachers and students are most familiar with, in some cases, all too familiar as students are asked to write "journals" for years with little or no instruction. It has been our experience that the teacher's role in journal writing is to comment on the bottom of the page and return it to the student. At its best, the journal provides a window into the child's life and creates an opportunity for the teacher and the student to engage in a personal conversation when there is little time for this in the press of classroom life. Most often, however, the student is locked into the journal form and, day after day, year after year, dutifully makes entries that are as prosaic and boring for the student to write as they are for the teacher to read. Without instruction in personal writing, journal writing, in this mode, does not move students forward in their ability to write expressively.

With anchor lessons teachers can extend "journals" and provide opportunities for students to write personal accounts with strength and voice.

If we look to the Writing Profile for Personal Recounts on page 30 for direction, we see that fully developed personal writing needs to show a strong point of view. It needs to express an opinion. Ideas and events are to be developed with supporting details and personal responses. From this we understand that a listing of events is insufficient. Unless the writing contains elements of personal reaction supported by details, examples and explanations, it is not a strong example of personal writing. As teachers of writing in this genre, it is up to us to make the elements of the genre explicit for our students. Let's look at two examples for clarity:

On June 11 we are having a field trip. We are going to the beach! We are not just going to play at the beach, but we are doing research there. I wonder if I'm going to find a starfish or a crab and if the water will be cold. I've been to the beach before so I know if there is sun it could be hot. I don't think I'm going to swim in the water but maybe . . . I can't wait!

By Kim

I get up in the morning and eat my breakfast. I brush my teeth and go to school. When I come into the classroom I hang my backpack on the hook and come to sit at the carpet. The teacher asks us if we have news. We can say yes or pass. Then we go to our chair and start our work.

By Winson

Kim gives us the pleasure of hearing her voice when she writes. We can delight in her excitement in anticipation of her trip. Kim's writing expresses a strong point of view and reaction. She is clearly engaged with her topic. Her writing expresses her individuality — it is vivid and she has chosen her language with care. Winson's work, on the other hand, has correct conventions, but it is a lacklustre list. There is little analysis and no personal reaction to the events of his day. We don't know Winson when we read his work.

Towards Powerful Personal Writing

When we teach students "Show, Don't Tell" in personal writing, they quickly see how it applies to poetry, narrative and nonfiction writing. The elements of each form of writing discussed in *Writing Anchors* are not necessarily unique to the form. There are many areas of overlap. These layers of overlap build student understanding across the dimensions of the four Writing Profiles.

Teachers can also help students understand the criteria for personal writing by highlighting good examples in read-alouds and by sharing their own personal writing, or samples from the class.

Students will submit personal writing like Winson's and the teacher, wanting something more, may prompt them by asking for "more." They then add details such as going out for recess, doing math and eating lunch. This is probably not the "more" the teacher is looking for.

In this chapter of *Writing Anchors*, we offer models of explicit instruction that unpack the dimensions of powerful personal writing. Our first lesson is designed to put an end to listing as Winson does above and invite students to supply supporting details with techniques such as "Zoom in." With explicit instruction, teachers show how to tell the inside and outside stories, demonstrating for students how characters respond to their situations. In later lessons, we provide opportunities for students to add details known only to the writer, to refine their personal accounts by using "Show, Don't Tell" and to revisit work to write leads that will hook the reader. These anchor lessons demonstrate for students how to engage with their topic, express an individual perspective, and choose their words with care.

Not only will students learn how to make their personal writing richer, but they will also learn how to generate and shape their ideas. For example, in these lessons we use cartooning and webbing.

Both teachers and students will enjoy the processes and the products of the personal writing anchor lessons.

Writing Profile for Personal Recounts

Dimensions of Writing	Undeveloped 1 At a Glance: The writing is brief, hard to understand and generic in tone.	2–3–4	Fully Developed 5 At a Glance: The writing is focused, expressive, easy to read and shows originality.
Engagement with the Topic • Meaning • Ideas • Details	Topic may be unclear or illogical; lacks a main idea. Writing is brief, with little development of ideas and few details or explanations.		Topic is focused and easy to read; the meaning is clear. Ideas are developed with relevant details, examples and explanations. The writer expresses a strong point of view. Writing may include personal feelings and opinions.
Vividness and Language Use • Energy • Passion • Voice • Word Choice • Variety • Expressiveness • Originality • Creativity	Writing provides stereotypical response to the topic and may contain clichés. The writer lacks energy and personal engagement. The voice of the writer is unclear — generic. Writing has no audience appeal in its current form. Language is simple. Writing lacks originality.		Writing is highly individual and expressive of the writer. The writer expresses energy for the topic. Rich and vivid language conveys details in the writer's own voice. The text has audience appeal — it would do well read aloud. Words are chosen for effect. The writer may experiment with poetic devices such as metaphor or simile. Sensory language is included. The writer takes risks to use language and expression in original ways.
Organization and Structure • Sequence • Clarity • Focus • Cohesion	Writing has little or no introduction. Writing loses focus; it is difficult to follow. There is a simple, repetitive sentence pattern. Ending may be abrupt.		Writing begins with an arresting lead. Ideas are easy to follow and cohesive; transition words are used effectively. Writing flows smoothly; it is clear and sequential. Sentence length and pattern are varied. Writing has a satisfying conclusion.
Conventions • Spelling • Punctuation • Grammar	Frequent errors in sentence structure, spelling, punctuation or grammar make the writing difficult to understand. Presentation is lacking care.		Basic sentence structure, grammar, spelling and punctuation are correct. There may be some errors on complex structures. Presentation shows care.

Zooming In on a Personal Moment

Why teach this anchor lesson?

- To show students how to engage with the topic and create vivid language by zooming in on one moment in time, telling the inside and outside stories, using dialogue to add impact, and telling details only the writer knows

How to do it

1. Inform students that they are going to use cartooning to zoom in on a personal experience in their life. They may choose an everyday moment, such as thinking as they lie in bed, losing keys, or discovering something, or a dramatic moment with lots of emotional impact, such as fighting with a sibling or going on a midway ride.
2. Model by recounting a personal experience or reading aloud from a piece of literature or one of the student samples included here. Explain what was happening — that's the outside story — and what the subject was thinking and feeling — or the inside story.
3. Ask students to practise using the technique of zooming in to tell the inside and outside stories of just one event in their life. Explain that the reader will want to experience the event the way they did and to read details only they know. They will need to magnify the moment to include the details.
4. Provide cartoon paper — sheets of paper folded in quarters — for each student. Ask students to sketch their ideas using thinking and speech bubbles that feature limited dialogue to make the moment come to life in the reader's mind.
5. Circulate, pausing to probe student thinking for details.

Special instructions: Prepare a sheet of paper folded in quarters for each student.

> **Remember the writing anchor: Zoom in!**

Janine recorded this instance of prompting a student to zoom in. "Tian Bo draws a series of pictures about going to Playdium with his family. He writes, 'I was going crazy because I was excited.' I see this as generic writing and so I asked him, 'What does going crazy look like and sound like? What did your father do?' Tian Bo thinks a moment and changes his writing to, 'I was so excited I was jumping up and down. I couldn't stop chattering. My father took hold of a little piece of my hair at the front and said, "Slow down."' Now I can see details only Tian Bo knows. The piece comes alive."

Student Reflection

- What does a powerful piece of personal writing need?
- What did you learn from this lesson that you can use in Writing Workshop?

Evaluation

To what extent was the student able to
- zoom in on one moment in time?
- tell the inside and outside stories?
- use dialogue to add impact?
- tells details only the writer knows?

Tracy's recount of her CorkScrew ride takes us right inside the moment, giving us the inside and the outside stories, so we experience the moment with the Grade 4 student.

In her account of her dad's search for the lost keys, Emma includes her own thoughts and feelings to expand the moment and take us with her into the story.

Lost and Found Keys
My dad lost his keys.
He cannot find them anywhere.
Are they under my bed,
In the toaster,
Or even in the oven?
Dad needs those keys to get to work.
He has to drive there
            FAST!
Without them he can't start the car
Or get into his building!
He needs to be there at 9:00 sharp
And it's already 8:00!
Dad has to leave in 15 minutes,
Or else he'll be late!
If he is late you don't want to know
What will happen!
Are the keys in the attic,
In a box?
I feel desperate.
My throat is dry.
I know I used those keys.
But I can't remember where!
Dad thinks I lost his keys.
Now he's yelling at me!
He needs those keys
What will he do?
He looks in his coat pocket
Even in his shoe!
He finally gives up
He can't find his keys
He looks down to tie his shoe
And finds the keys on a cord
Around his neck.

Wasn't That Fun?

I couldn't believe it! I was actually going to do it! I was lining up for the Cork Screw. I was wide eyed staring at the gigantic ride. High above me was endless hoops, turns, jerks, hills, loops, and twirls. My heart, I could feel pounding. "I chose to go on this, but why?" I asked myself. So I could get out of this terrible situation, I closed my eyes.

In my head I could imagine myself taking steps toward home. Suddenly, Alex yelled, "Good luck!" I was two people away from my worst night mare. Two passengers then I could be on board. I'd been chattering my teeth now for the past 20 minutes. They hurt, so did my knees. They had been knocking together since the last time I checked my watch.

Someone pushed my back. I looked back but no one was there. "Oh well" I thought aloud. While I was thinking about who pushed me someone latched me up! I looked around. I was trapped in the bars! I tried to escape the huge ride by closing my eyes. I was bumping up and down very slowly. We were going up the hill bump. Bump. Bump. I looked up for a moment at the sky to wish that I would have a safe journey. I said to myself It can't be that bbbbbaaadddddd HELP ME!!!! I was taking the long journey down.

Then we started the endless curves and bumps. We went straight. Then to the left! Then to the right! Then up. Then down. And to the right. Then left!

Oh no! We were coming up to the . . . Upside down, screaming, yelling, gasping for air loop da loop. Upside down! Twice! Straight, straight, straight, loop, loop around and around again. My head was spinning — and fast. Again up we went suddenly! I held onto my head thinking it might come off. I couldn't take it any more! Then we slowly went down the hill. Straight. Straight.

I could see people waiting in line. It slides. Then halts. It's over. I quietly sigh with relief. Terror loosened its grip from my shoulders from everyone begging me to go on. I had done it. I was a survivor. I got off the ride still scared, but proud. Then Alex, Jenny, and Zarhra came up and to me and hollered, "Wasn't that fun?"

By Tracy

In this piece, Jessie (Grade 3) layers the details that only she can know to create the setting for her bedtime thoughts.

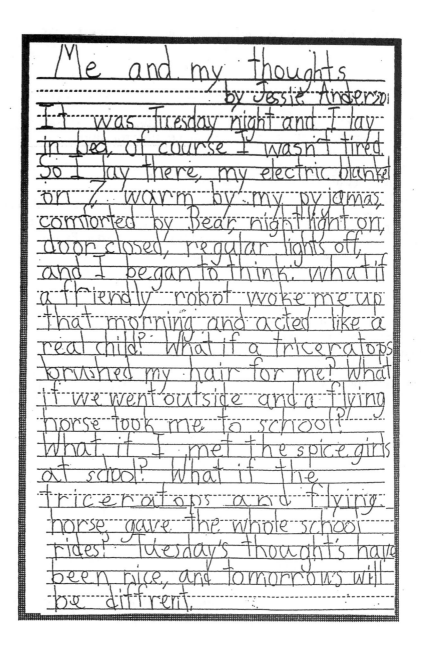

Me and my thoughts
by Jessie Anderson

It was Tuesday night and I lay in bed. of course I wasn't tired. So I lay there, my electric blanket on 7. warm by my pyjamas, comforted by Bear, night light on, door closed, regular lights off, and I began to think. what if a friendly robot woke me up that morning and acted like a real child? What if a triceratops brushed my hair for me? What if we went outside and a flying horse took me to school? What if I met the spice girls at school? What if the triceratops and flying horse, gave the whole school rides? Tuesday's thoughts have been nice, and tomorrows will be diffrent.

Scaffolding Recount with Smooth Transitions

This lesson focuses on transition words for sequencing events in time. We have also included an exhaustive blackline master of other transition words (BLM 2.1). We invite teachers to select the ones appropriate to their grade to put on a chart to use for future lessons.

Special instructions: Select words from the chart given under #2 and record on the chalkboard or on a chart for student reference. The words should be appropriate to the students' grade level.

Why teach this anchor lesson?

- To show students how to organize and structure their work using vocabulary related to time transitions: e.g., *first, next, then*.

How to do it

1. Engage students in a conversation about an experience they have in common, perhaps a field trip or a special event in the class. Ask students to list the events in order. Explain that they will learn to do a recount of events in order. For example:

   We got on the bus   We went into the arena
   We drove to Trout Lake
      Arena for skating   We sat down and put on our skates
   etc.

2. Introduce the chart of transition words, as shown below. Explain to students that fully developed writing has transitions that are easy for the reader to follow. Events flow in a logical sequence from one to the next often using words such as those on the chart.

to begin with	first	in the meantime	at the same time
concurrently	simultaneously	at this point	meanwhile
afterwards	later	after	second
third	fourth	subsequently	then
next	soon	finally	in the end
following that	last	then	before
within minutes	now	previously	immediately
later	as time passed		
soon	eventually		

3. In the case of a recount, the opening sentences not only have to draw the reader in, they also orient the reader to the topic. They explain who, what, where, when and why the event occurs. Engage students in developing appropriate opening sentences. For example: We're off! On Tuesday, Feb. 10, students at Maquinna Annex School raced for the bus and skating at Trout Lake Arena.

4. Ask students to consider the list of events they have developed and to select two or three transition words that they can use to relate some of the events in sequence. Students talk to a partner about events in order, using the words and phrases for transitions. Select some students to share their examples.

5. Explain to students that, as it stands, they have a list or an outline, not a fully developed personal account. With students "flesh out" one of the events into a paragraph using techniques they have learned, for example, zooming in. Explain to students that they need to add the details so the reader can visualize the experience.

It may be too much for younger students to learn transitions and the opening sentence in one lesson. Teachers may decide to revisit the writing to add information about opening sentences.

6. Demonstrate how the transition words are to be incorporated into what they know about powerful writing to create a sense of flow in the recount. (Older students may understand that each transition could begin a new paragraph.)
7. Students finish writing their recount of the event, adding details and using transition words appropriately.

Remember the writing anchor: Make smooth transitions.

Student Reflection

- Where were you able to use transition words without creating a list? Read your favorite section to a partner.
- What will you remember about transition words in your own writing?
- What will you remember about writing a recount of events?

Evaluation

To what extent was the student able to
– open with interesting information that orients the reader to the topic?
– develop the topic with details that help the reader to visualize the experience?
– use a variety of transition words to sequence events?

The Friday Journal: A Personal Recount with Details

The Friday Journal is a letter to parents written by their child explaining the events enjoyed most during the week at school. It provides an opportunity for students to practise "Zoom in" and it lets parents see the child's progress in unedited work. The parents are requested to reply with details from their own lives at school. (See the letter to parents on page 37.)

Why teach this anchor lesson?

- To show students how to engage with the topic and create vivid language by zooming in on a moment, telling the inside and outside stories, using dialogue to add impact, and telling details only the writer knows

How to do it

1. Explain to students that each Friday they will be writing a letter to their parents in a book called The Friday Journal. They will take it home on Friday to show their parents and return it to school on Monday. Parents are requested to write to their children and tell about something that happened in their week or in their life at school.
2. Brainstorm things that have happened in school this week.
3. Review the criteria for powerful personal writing:

   - Zoom in on a moment.
   - Tell the inside and outside stories.
   - Use dialogue to add impact.
   - Tell details only the writer knows.
   - Use transition words appropriately.

   You might work with the class with an example, such as this used with young students: "This week I played in the snow with my friends. We also made a snow poem. We are studying about space." Discuss the writing in relation to the criteria. Once the class decides that this writing does not meet the criteria, work together to make improvements, for example:

   This week I played in the snow with my friends. We worked together to make a huge snowman. We used stones for the face. Tracey let us use her scarf and we put it around the snowman's neck. When we were finished, our snowman looked very funny and we felt proud.

   Now the students can see how to make their writing more powerful.
4. Remind students not to write a list of all the events of the week, but rather to pick a focus and meet the criteria for powerful personal writing.

The Friday Journal is also a great place for teaching students about paragraphing, opening sentences and great closings. It is a complete piece done in one sitting. It clearly demonstrates the student's progress over time and provides evidence of craft lessons learned.

> Remember the writing anchors: Zoom in! Tell the inside and outside stories.

Student Reflection

- What did you enjoy most this week?
- What parts of your work meet the criteria for personal writing? Share them with a partner.

Evaluation

To what extent was the student able to
– zoom in on a moment ?
– tell the inside and outside stories?
– use dialogue to add impact?
– tell details only the writer knows?
– use transitions appropriately?

Letter to Parents About the Friday Journal

(Date)

Dear Parents,

This book is called the "Friday Journal." In it, your son or daughter will write a letter to you each week describing one or two of the things we did in class during the week. I will be correcting the Friday Journal minimally so that you will have an opportunity to see your child's unedited writing development. I know you will be pleased to see the growth over the year.

In addition to the letter in the Friday Journal, there will frequently be a math activity for your student to do with the family. These math activities will reflect the current topics of study in the math class. Please participate with your child in these activities.

Finally, I want the children to enjoy writing the Friday Journal and sharing it with their parents. You know how discouraging it is to write to a friend who never writes back. You can help me at home by writing a note to your child each week in response to the Journal. You may write in English or a language of your choice.

Please, take a few moments to write a message of encouragement in the Friday Journal.

Sincerely,

Sophie's letter shows her creativity and an original response to the Friday Journal assignment. Her detailed drawings describe her work in school that week and provide a starting point for a conversation with her dad.

Apr. 9

Hi Mom and Dad!
This letter log is going to be quite different, because it's only going to be illustrations! No captions! I'm just going to add lots of detail to my picture, so you can guess what we've been doing. I'll be doing two for each subject, and there will be 4 subjects. I hope you enjoy the pictures! You might be able to guess everything we're doing!
Bye,
From Sophie

Science

Needs to be repaired!   Repaired

Math

Which sides are congruent?

Which solid will this net make?

Dancing with Desiree

Legend:
△ = Center center
▪ = Down stage
⊙ = Up stage
▪R = Downstage right
▪L = Downstage left
⊙L = Upstage left
⊙R = Upstage right

Penny toss game

Art

Dear Sophie,

I learned some new things from your drawings. I did not know about up stage and down stage and the history about stages. Thank you for telling me about it.

I could not remember what congruent meant, until you reminded me.

The electrical circuits are useful new things to learn. Your art works is great.

Love, Dad

Collections: Adding Detail from Personal Experience

This anchor lesson provides rich and authentic opportunities for students to write. If you include the recommended "Collections Day," it could easily take a week. The original idea for the lesson comes from teacher Carollyne Sinclaire.

Byrd Baylor's story *Everybody Needs a Rock* is an excellent complement to this lesson.

Why teach this anchor lesson?

- To show students how to engage with the topic and create vivid language by using dialogue to add impact and telling details only the writer knows
- To tell the reader how to follow a procedure to reach a goal

How to do it

1. Bring in a collection to share with the class. Show your collection and tell the students how you select items, where the items have been found or acquired, how you arrange or keep the collection, what it means to you, how you got started, and what special features your collection has.
2. Discuss any collections the students might have. Collections include such items as coins, toys, erasers, ornaments, tickets, mugs, and key chains. Anything goes! You'll be surprised what students collect.
3. Organize "Collections Day." Invite the students to bring their collections to school. They set up their collections on their desks. Divide the class into two groups. Half stay at their stations and talk about their collections while the others visit and ask questions. Then they reverse roles. If there is anyone without a collection, partner him or her with a friend. Take photographs of the students with their collections before the students carefully put them away.
4. Explain to students that they are going to write "Ten Rules for Collecting." Remind students that personal writing needs to show strong connections to the writer's own experience.
5. Model for students what is meant by adding more detail. For example, a student writes, "You need a shelf to put your stuffed animals on." Write this on the blackboard or chart paper, and prompt the class much like this: "Tell me more about the size of the shelf. Is it large or small? Where is it? Why do you need a shelf rather than a box or a basket? What else might be important about this shelf?" As the students make suggestions, add them to the blackboard or chart. Here's what the revised version might look like:

   You need a shelf to display your animals. Not too high or it won't be seen. Not too low because your little brother or sister might be able to get them. Eye level is just right. The shelf should be wide enough so they are not too crowded so each one can have some space to breathe. Your stuffed animals will thank you for giving them a space of their own.

6. Students set to work listing their 10 rules for collecting and then supplying more detail and tips for the collector to get it just right.
7. Share in partners. Make adding more detail a focus for conferences.
8. Students edit for spelling and make good copies to display on a bulletin board next to the photos taken.

Student Reflection

- How did your writing change from your first list of rules to your final copy?
- Which rule do you think demonstrates the criteria for this activity best?
- What did you learn in this lesson that you can apply to Writing Workshop?

Evaluation

To what extent was the student able to
– use details from personal experience to create an impact on the reader?
– tell the reader how to follow a procedure to reach a goal?
– use the technique of speaking directly to the reader?

Collection of Marbles

1. It has to have a shiny sparkle in the sunlight.
2. It can't have a chip in it or it won't look good and it won't roll very well.
3. You have to look at it like a dragon with glowing red eyes and blowing fire.
4. You must ask yourself — do I like it? and does it suit me?
5. It has to be as smooth as a crystal star in a foggy night.
6. You have to collect many different colours and sizes.
7. If you play against someone use the one marble that is not most special.
8. Try and collect as many marbles as you can.
9. End the game as good friends.
10. Play fairly.

By Jacob

My Collection of Poetry

1. The first rule is you have to go to the back of your mind where all your different thoughts are.
2. Don't write a poem because you want to pass time. Write it because you need a new way of expressing yourself.
3. You have to write according to your feelings. If you're mad, write a poem that shows it. If you're sad write a poem about it. You can do the same with all your feelings.
4. Don't write for other people. If they want to write they should know what to write about.
5. It's important you can see what you're going to write. Not like you can see the blackboard or your deskmate, but see it in your mind's eye.
6. To have a good poetry collection, you need to think about what you write. That way you always know if you really want to write this poem.
7. To have a good collection you have to have variety. There are many different kinds of poems: Haiku, limericks, diamante and many more.
8. You really should write more than one version of a poem. For example, if you write about a family trip, write a limerick and a diamante poem. That way you have more than one poem about it.

9. *A good place to keep a poem is in your head. You can also print it on the computer. Then make up a book of it. That way it's easier to transport.*
10. *The final and most important rule is you must be able to feel a poem not with your hands but with your heart.*

By Sarah

Show, Don't Tell: My Teacher

Why teach this anchor lesson?

- To show students how to engage with the topic, create vividness by conveying emotion "between the lines" in the details and make effective word choice, in other words, to introduce the Show, Don't Tell technique

How to do it

1. Ask the class to suggest the name of someone they all know to write about.
2. The following is an example of how the writing teacher would lead the class to understanding how to apply the Show, Don't Tell technique.

   TEACHER: Let's start with Ms Sleep. We all know her well. Tell me about Ms Sleep.

   STUDENTS: She's fun.

   TEACHER: I agree. Ms Sleep is fun. I want to show you how to take out the word "fun" and still let the reader know that she is fun. Let's try this together. What does Ms Sleep do that is fun?

   The teacher begins a web on the board. She titles the web "Ms Sleep" and puts "FUN" in the centre of the web. As the students brainstorm examples of Ms Sleep's fun-loving spirit, the teacher writes them on the spokes of the web. Using the examples from the web they craft the following together:

   When we came inside from a snowy recess Ms Sleep had hot cocoa with marshmallow on top waiting for us. She helped us out of our soggy clothes and told us to warm our red hands around the sides of the cup until it was cool enough to drink. At Christmas time Ms Sleep brought us each a Christmas tree cookie and green icing and Smarties to decorate it. She just laughed and her blue eyes sparkled when we were greedy and piled the icing on thick to hold too many candies. Last month we had Aerobathon. Ms Sleep came with her skinny legs sticking out of her wide shorts and gave us a challenge. She called out to the whole school, "Anyone who can run as many laps as I can will come to the park with me for a lemonade lunch!" . . . the race was on!

   TEACHER: Do you see how our story is more powerful than saying, "Ms Sleep is fun"? That is what I mean by show, don't tell. We can show by examples what someone or something is like.

3. Ask the students to think of a person they know and a word to describe them. Examples: Dad— joker; Mom — thoughtful.

Our colleague, Brenda Boylan, does a daily activity with Show, Don't Tell. She writes a "telling" sentence on the board and engages the class in rewriting it to "show." For example:

Telling: Moatia was sad when she walked to school.
Showing: Moatia's shoulders drooped, her backpack hung loosely from one arm, the bottom dragging on the road. Moatia walked slowly to school, kicking at a pebble in her path.

The student writes, "My dad plays stuff with me." The teacher pauses to ask, "What's stuff? Tell us exactly what your dad plays with you. Everybody's dad plays "stuff" — that's a generic term. Tell the story so it can only be *your* dad." The student writes: "Whenever we go to the adventure playground my dad plays Pirates and the Treasure with me. We pretend that the culvert is a pirate hideout and we have to tiptoe past to get the gold." The teacher responds, "Yes, now I see. Your dad has a great imagination! That's specific and it could only be your dad."

These student samples show how Kim and Delaney reveal what their fathers are like without relying on adjectives.

4. Engage students in a discussion about people they know and their qualities. Ask students to turn and share their thoughts with partners in response to the following prompts:

   - Who is the person you are thinking of?
   - Which one quality will you choose to describe?
   - What are some of the things the person does to show that quality?

5. Students write using Show, Don't Tell. They can begin by putting the name of the person at the top of a web. In the centre of the web they put the quality they want to write about. Around the spokes of the web, they list examples.
6. Circulate and prompt students to think of specific, not generic examples.
7. Students meet to share their drafts informally.

Remember the writing anchor: Show, don't tell.

Student Reflection

- What is your favorite Show, Don't Tell example? Read it out loud for your partner.
- What did you learn in the lesson today that you can use in Writing Workshop?

Evaluation

To what extent was the student able to
– convey meaning through specific examples?

My Dad

My Dad helps me with math whenever I have homework. He takes me to Toys R Us and gives me ideas for games to get. He makes pizza and birdhouses for me. He even does my hair for special occasions and helps me make birthday cards for my friends.

By Kim

Daddy

Daddy, thank you for staying up with me last night when I was sick. Thank you for taking us out for dinner when Mom's away. Sometimes in the spring you take us biking. Brave Dad, you had to take us out swimming by 4:00 and we got out of school at 3:05. You are so brave! I love you.

By Delaney

Special Places

Why teach this anchor lesson?

- To demonstrate the power of rehearsing with a sketch or a map to help students visualize the story
- To consolidate lessons in personal writing taught so far, including zooming in on a moment, telling the inside and outside stories, using dialogue to add impact, telling details only the writer knows, creating impact on the reader with details from personal experience, and using the Show, Don't Tell technique

How to do it

As an alternative to telling a personal story, read an example from children's literature. Some suggested titles are *Owl Moon* by Jane Yolen and *Where the Forest Meets the Sea* by Jeannie Baker. A second alternative would be to read aloud one of the student samples provided.

1. Tell a story about a special place that means a lot to you. It could be a memory from childhood about a special place where you played with a friend or sibling, a place you visited with your parents, a memory of a vacation or just a memory of a place that you remember fondly. Keep it short, but make the point that the place was somewhere where you were happy. You know things about this place that no one else will know. It means something special to you.
2. Instruct students to close their eyes and imagine a place that is very special for them. Guide their thinking. Talk about where this place might be (at home, at Grandma's house, at the beach, in the park, at a favorite vacation spot). When they have chosen the place, ask them to open their eyes and draw a map or picture of the place. Have them work in silence.

   Continue to prompt their thinking: "Are you alone? Who is in the place with you? What can you hear? What can you see?" Emphasize that this is a sketch, not a complete picture. Give no more than 10 minutes to the drawing.
3. Students share their sketch with a partner and tell their story about their special place.
4. Students begin to draft their work. Circulate, pausing to offer help, probe students' thinking and highlight powerful examples.
5. Students meet informally to share their writing.

> Remember the writing anchors: Zoom in! Make it your own! Tell details only the writer knows.

Student Reflection

- What did you enjoy about this writing time today?
- Choose the passages from your work that best exemplify the criteria we are working on in personal writing.
- What will you use from this lesson in Writing Workshop?

Evaluation

To what extent was the student able to
– write with a sense of personal voice in the piece?
– reflect their own experience?
– use detail to make an impact on the reader?

Clarissa's sketch shows details that later the Grade 4 student will include in her writing.

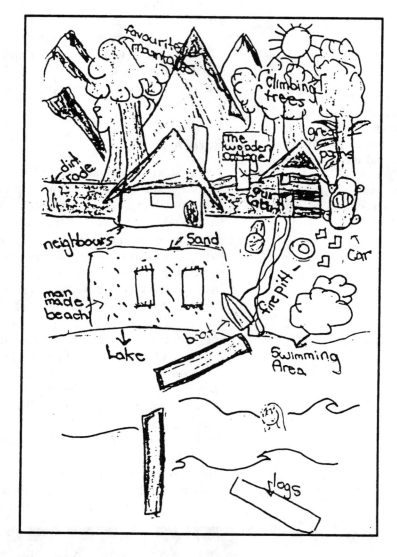

By Clarissa

Alison writes about a special place where she goes to hide "to think my own thoughts in privacy." Notice how she includes sensory details: the bumpy floor, rough on her hands; the smell, musty but also homey like a "big hug"; the sounds from the kitchen of pots and pans as dinner is made. The Grade 5 student takes us in our imaginations to the old closet through her use of detail.

The Old Closet

The old closet floor is bumpy with jagged, sticking up nails. It feels rough on my hands. It smells musty and old but somehow it has a strong homey feeling like it's putting its arms around me in a big hug. The old closet is relaxing. The walls are white washed and the rods and shelves neatly stuffed with clothes and games. The only sounds you can hear when the closet door is shut are the bumps and clangs of pots while dinner is being made. I go there to think my own thoughts in privacy. I'm going there now.

By Alison

Allison's special place is about playing a game with her cousins. The Grade 3 student describes how to play the game with the balloons. The fun she is having is shared with the reader in the invitation, "Would you like to come to my special place? I have a balloon waiting for you."

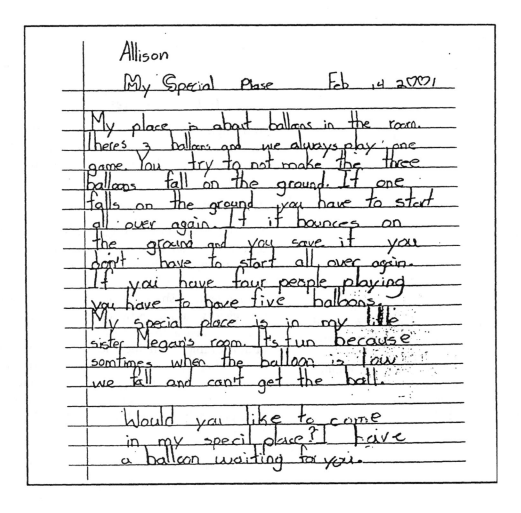

Allison

My Special Plase   Feb 14 2001

My place is about ballons in the room. Theres 3 ballons and we always play one game. You try to not make the three balloons fall on the ground. If one falls on the ground you have to start all over again. If it bounces on the ground and you save it you don't have to start all over again. If you have four people playing you have to have five ballons. My special place is in my litle sister Megan's room. Its fun because somtimes when the balloon is low we fall and can't get the ball.

Would you like to come in my specil place? I have a balloon waiting for you.

Find a Hook

Why teach this anchor lesson?

- To strengthen student writing on the dimension of Engagement with the Topic by creating a strong opening
- To show students that good writers often revisit their work to polish it

How to do it

1. Ask students to look through the books in their independent reading collection for opening sentences that draw them in and make them want to keep reading. Provide sticky notes or markers so students can bring their examples to the lesson. (Tip: Magazine articles often have great openings.)
2. Ask students to share examples from their search. As they do so, ask students to suggest what makes the opening powerful. They will discover that effective leads may give a hint of a mystery or intrigue, ask a question, spring from the middle of the action, include a quotation, include a sound effect, start with an amazing fact or set a mood. They hook the reader.
3. Revisit a piece of writing the class has done together in a previous lesson with a view to rewriting the opening to make it stronger. In the following example, we have used the piece about Ms Sleep in Show, Don't Tell: My Teacher.

Depending on the age of the students, you may want to spread this lesson out over several days. Perhaps your group could have a series of mini-lessons in Writing Workshop and apply each type of opening to a new piece or revisit a finished piece.

> When we came inside from a snowy recess Ms Sleep had hot cocoa with marshmallow on top waiting for us. She helped us out of our soggy clothes and told us to warm our red hands around the sides of the cup until it was cool enough to drink. At Christmas time Ms Sleep brought us each a Christmas tree cookie and icing and smarties to decorate it. She just laughed and her blue eyes sparkled when we were greedy and piled the icing on thick to hold way too many candies. Last month we had Aerobathon. Ms Sleep came in her wide shorts with her skinny legs sticking out and she gave us a challenge. She called out to the whole school, "Anyone who can do as many laps and I can will come to the park with me for a lemonade lunch!" . . . the race was on!

4. Engage students in experimenting with new openings. While you write, think aloud and experiment with each type of opening sentence.

> ## What Does an Effective Opening Do?
>
> - Gives a hint of a mystery that makes the reader want more information—*As I entered the classroom, a sweet smell greeted me.*
> - Asks a question—*Is your teacher full of fun? You should meet Ms Sleep.*
> - Springs from the middle of the action—*The bell rang just as we finished the snowman.*
> - Includes a quotation—*"Who wants hot cocoa?" Ms Sleep called.*
> - Includes a sound effect—*"Buzz!" Recess is over. Good thing 'cause I'm freezing.*
> - Starts with an amazing fact—*Hot cocoa and snow go well together.*
> - Sets the mood—*With teeth chattering from the cold, sodden snowpants weighing us down we slopped in from recess.*

5. Ask students to select a piece of writing that they have already finished to revise the opening in one of the ways learned.

Remember the writing anchor: Find a hook.

Student Reflection

- Share your revised opening(s) with your partner and explain which type of hook you used.
- What did you learn today that you can use in Writing Workshop?

Evaluation

To what extent was the student able to
– create a strong opening?
– identify different ways to hook the reader?

> ### Anchor Lessons Based on Response to Literature
>
> One aspect of personal writing that many teachers use in the language arts program is response to literature. Typically, students read books independently and then respond in their journals in open-ended ways, commenting on what they liked, how they made connections with the text, and what they felt about the story. These journals may be used in literature circles, where small groups of students meet to share ideas about books.
>
> There are many different ways to engage students in responding to literature, but as with all classroom assignments, their writing can be improved with teacher demonstration, guided practice and feedback, and ways of scaffolding the response. The open-ended instruction to write about what the book made you feel often results in the generic "I liked it. It was good." In the anchor lessons in this next section, we make some suggestions for ways to include response to literature in Writing Workshop.
>
> All these ideas depend on the organization of students into book clubs or literature circles, composed of members who have read the same text. The discussion that takes place in these groups is part of the process. Students may write *before* the discussion, *after* the discussion, or both, moving back and forth between talk and writing. We suggest here that part of Writing Workshop should be anchor lessons on what makes an effective, well-crafted and powerful response. A colleague, Lisa House, helped us develop a rubric to assess student response to literature and tried it with her students in Grades 8 and 9. We include it as Blackline Master 2.2. It provides the basis for criteria setting and evaluation.

Recounting or Retelling a Story

Why teach this anchor lesson?

· To scaffold reader response by starting with the most literal
· To increase student awareness of the structure of stories and so help their own story writing
· To develop students' ability to synthesize information

How to do it

1. Students read a story or a chapter from a novel. They meet in groups and in discussion summarize what they have read. They may summarize the beginning, the middle and the ending sections using the language of transitions: *first*, *then*, and *finally*. Alternatively, they may summarize a special section of the text, perhaps the scariest, the funniest or the saddest.
2. After the discussion, the teacher calls the whole class together, and using an overhead transparency, creates a communal synopsis of the shared text, focusing on main ideas and important supporting details, and eliminating the least important information. The summary will convey information about the most important themes in the story. If appropriate, it will show awareness of character motivation.
3. Students then practise this skill as they read and retell another short story or chapter from their novel. They share their writing in a literature circle, each taking a turn to read their synopsis.

> Remember the writing anchor: Find the keys.

Student Reflection

· How did you decide what to include and what to leave out of your summary?
· How did recounting the story help you to understand it better?
· Did the themes and characters in the story become clearer?

Evaluation

The retelling could also be done in role as a character from the story. For more details see the writing-in-role lesson on pages 144–45.

Gabriele identifies with a mother owl.

To what extent was the student able to
– show awareness of major themes or character motivation?
– to synthesize the main ideas and eliminate extraneous detail?

I am a Great Grey Owl

I am a Great Grey Owl. I am a proud nocturnal creature who sleeps in the day and hunts at night. I find my food. Wait! I hear something in the grass! It's a mouse quivering with fright. I am a mighty owl. I see the mouse and that will be my rodent meal. I glide and go down. I swoop to get the mouse. I strike! My talons grab the mouse and I eat. I spit the pellet out. Now I give food to my babies when they are hungry. Time to sleep till nightfall returns and it's time to prey.

By Gabrielle

Here is a Grade 5 student's retelling of the story *Wolf* by Becky Bloom.

Wolf

"Oh, I'm so hungry" wolf groaned. Wolf groaned as he walked around town with an empty stomach. "I know, I'll visit the farm!" he said. As the Wolf walked to the farm, he was shocked to see farm animals reading. "Oh, my imagination's playing tricks on me again" he said. But, it wasn't his imagination. Wolf jumped over the fence and howled. "What's that noise? Can't they be quiet here?" Duck asked. The wolf was shocked to know that farm animals like us aren't scared of him. "What? Why aren't you scared of me?" he asked. "Can't you see? We're reading here." I replied. "Can you pleas go now? We're reading here." Pig said as he gave wolf a little push outside. "What's wrong, why aren't they scared of me?" Wolf asked himself on his way out. "Oh, I know! I'll go to school!" he suggested. The teacher and the kids were frightened to see a wolf in their classroom. After a lot of work, Wolf finally learned how to read and write.

The following day, Wolf walked in the farm and tried to amuse us by reading his book. Wolf read sentence to sentence. "I think you can do better then that" Duck interrupted. Wolf was confused, how can he read better than that? Soon enough, Wolf decided to practice reading in the Library. He read every book and couldn't take his eyes off them. "After a lot of reading, I think I'm ready now" he said.

Meanwhile, Wolf knocked on the door with a book by his side. As soon as he walked in, he read as fast as he could. "I think you need some style" I suggested. Wolf walked outside with his book. "What style?" He asked over and over to his self. Suddenly, he thought of an idea. "I know! I'll buy my own book!" he yelled with excitement. With the little money he had. Wolf bought his very first own book. Wolf read his book every night.

As soon as Wolf reached the farm, he rang the doorbell and walked in. Wolf read his very own book, until duck, Pig and I were amused by his reading. Wolf read lots and lots of stories until, "do you want to join us in our picnic later?" I asked. "Sure, why not!" he replied.

Later on, everyone ate and read their books. "You know, we can be professional story readers" I suggested. "And travel around the world!" Pig continued. "We can start tomorrow!" Duck replied. Soon enough, all four of us became professional story readers.

The Gift of Words

Special instructions: Prepare some strips of paper on which are written Gifts of Words from a story. Gifts of Words can show literary language such as metaphor, simile and onomatopoeia. They can also be descriptive, exciting, poignant or especially meaningful. Have available chart paper and marker pens.

Why teach this anchor lesson?

- To increase students' awareness of literary language
- To develop a greater sensitivity towards vocabulary and the meaning of words

How to do it

1. Share a story with the class. Model what is meant by a Gift of Words. Show how the author has made deliberate word choices. Explain that these are a gift from the writer to the reader.
2. Talk about the Gifts of Words you have chosen and why you chose them.
3. On large chart paper using felt markers, the students work cooperatively in pairs to retell the story. Partner talk aids the retelling. Students must incorporate the Gifts of Words that you have provided on the strips of paper by pasting them into the text they are creating. To help younger students, or those who need more help, photocopy three or four key images to help them structure their retelling.

Remember the writing anchor: Play with words!

Student Reflection

- Which was your favorite Gift of Words and why?
- How did having the Gifts of Words help you to write your version of the story?

Evaluation

To what extent was the student able to
– incorporate the Gifts of Words into the reading in a meaningful way?

Three Extensions

1. Students may collect Gifts of Words as they read and record them in their reading journals. They could respond to the passages, describing the thoughts, images or feelings that they evoke, and then share these in their literature circles. Below is a Grade 6 student example.

From "Fox":

"Fox with his haunted eyes and rich red coat. He flickers through the trees like a tongue of fire and Magpie trembles."

I liked this piece of language more than the others because of the image it creates in my mind. A flash of red here, a dash of it there, it reminds me of the book, "Chasing Redbird." All you see is that flicker of red, just like fire, and the eyes! Sorrow, loneliness and envy is what one would see when looking into those

---

magnificent eyes. The rage of living a lifetime of lonesomeness, waiting, feeling, and breathing as a mere dart of red . . . beautiful and respected red, not the sort to befriend.

By Chloe

2. Ask students to select words and phrases from a piece of literature that engages them. They then arrange the words and elaborate with their own ideas to create a found poem. Below is a student sample inspired by Thomas Locker's *Water Dance*.

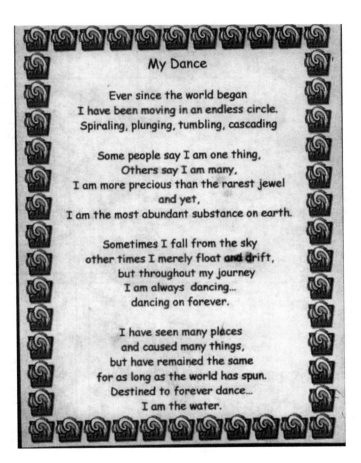

3. As an alternative way of responding to a story, have students choose a character from a story that you read aloud and write a letter to another character. To prepare students for the activity, read aloud a story that has emotional impact without sharing the pictures. Stop the reading four times to allow students to sketch what they visualize and to jot down words they want to remember. Discuss the images and language after each interval. Students could use Blackline Master 2.3 to help retell the story. Our colleague, Carrie Sleep, developed this method of scaffolding.

Four sketches and the selection of key words helped plan the next piece of writing. Note how this young Grade 3 writer conveys an understanding of the character's feelings.

Name: Delaney   Title: The Crane wife   Author: _____   Date: _____

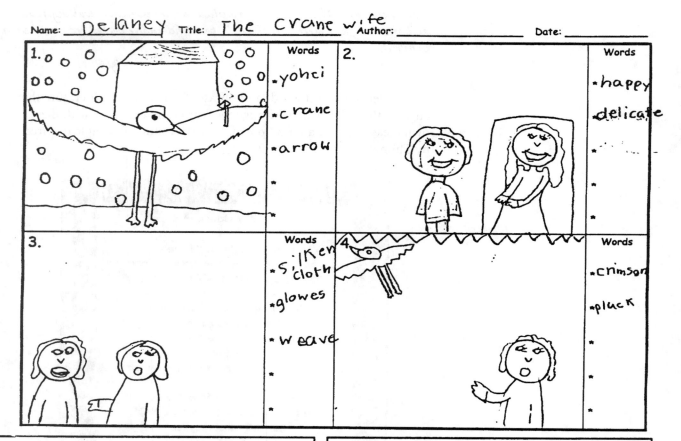

1.
Words
*yohei
*crane
*arrow
*

2.
Words
*happy
delicate
*
*

3.
Words
*silken cloth
*glowes
*weave
*

4.
Words
*crimson
*pluck
*

April 22, 2003

Dear Yohei
I remember when you found me on the ground lying wounded that's when I fell in loved with your gentle kind heart. We're happy together when were first married. but. Why then you only care about money? Money money money Why can't you be as kind as before? like the time where I am would my body filling with pain, why are you so curious peeking thorgh the door now were apart. The second time I weave I tol you it was the very very last time but Why did you beg me? Your brian is only thinking about money all about money did you even care about me? If you did you won't ask me one more time to weave, I don't think you really care about me Yohei. Yohei if you have another wife don't treat her as you did to me or else she will leave you. Dont just think about money think about caring about people I just hope that you have learnd a lesson!

From: Your Wife .

the crane wife
Dear crane wife, I remembered when you fell and got shot. I hope you forgive me for looking at you I hope I will stay in your heart. I will always remember you in my heart, I remember how kind and gentle you were. I will also remember how exquisite, delikite silkin, gold and shiney your patterns were. Ad you a nod sacrifice to see you do all of that for me just for me I hope you'll write me back Please come and visit me again. You were a very very very very very nice women. I fainted when I saw all the blood but I will still love you always and you will still remain in my heart. I will always think about you and how goneros you were to me. It was a good knowing you crane wife Please remember me onece more. And you gold exquiste patterns were very very prettyand lovly. and butiful.

52

Connecting

Why teach this anchor lesson?

- To increase students' ability to connect literature to their own experience, thus deepening their understanding of the text

How to do it

1. Model the process of making connections to a story by commenting on your own personal connections as you read aloud. You can make connections to things that have happened to you, to things you know about but have not actually experienced, or to other books and stories. Films and videos and music may also form part of the landscape of personal connection.
2. Give the students a story to read, or assign a chapter from their novel. Explain that they are to stop and notice whenever the story reminds them of something they have experienced. They can record these connections on sticky notes and place them on the page.
3. In the literature circle, ask students to share their connections.
4. Finally, assign a writing activity in which the students explore the story they have read through the lens of their personal connections. Sentence starters can be especially helpful for this. Some suggestions follow:

   - This makes me think of (a story like this one) because . . .
   - This makes me think of (a time when something like this happened to me)
   - This makes me think of (something I know about the world)

> Remember the writing anchors: Make it your own! Tell details only the writer knows. Tell the inside and outside stories.

Student Reflection

- How did thinking about your own experiences help you to understand the characters in the story?
- What did you learn about the story by making your own connections to it?

Evaluation

To what extent was the student able to
- make insightful connections to personal ideas, opinions, experiences and feelings that help develop conclusions about the text?
- draw upon a repertoire of reading, viewing and listening to make connections?

In this response to the story of White Lily by Ting-Xing Ye, the student relates the story to her own feelings and thinks about how her family would behave if she was in pain.

White Lily

Feb. 6.

I was shocked when White Lily's mom and grandma bound White Lily's feet like that! If I was hurt my parents wouldn't do that. My parents would help me up not leave me in pain. I'm still wondering why Jui-Gui was not there to help his sister bear the pain in her legs. My favorite part so far is when it was White Lily's father's birthday, she recited a poem for her father how sweet. On chapter 8 page 33 it says, Next morning after a festive breakfast of steamed stick-rice cakes molded into animal shapes, and boiled round dumplings stuffed fat with sweet red bean paste reminded me when it was new years and I went for Dim Sum. YUM!

It was a different time

Great job.

Reflecting and Evaluating

Why teach this anchor lesson?

- To assist students in forming opinions and expressing their original ideas
- To help them think ahead, or predict the outcome of a story

How to do it

1. Provide sentence starters for the response writing that focus on evaluating the meaning of the story. Here are some suggestions:

   - This story makes me feel _____ because . . .
   - I used to think _____ but now I _____
   - I wonder . . .
   - In my opinion . . .
   - I understand why _____, but I think _____
   - The message I think the author wanted us to understand is . . .
   - Questions I have for the author (or character) are . . .
   - I understand the story to mean . . .
   - This story will change the way I _____ because _____

2. The students write a response either after the story is complete, or during the story, allowing for predictions to be made based on unfolding evidence from the text. Encourage them to use quotations and reference the text accurately. These responses are used in the literature circle to clarify understandings and develop further inferences about the meaning.

Remember the writing anchor: Make it your own!

Student Reflection

- How did writing about your opinions help you understand the author's point of view?
- Did you have questions for the author? If so, did they help you clarify your understanding?

Evaluation

To what extent was the student able to
- show through writing an awareness of the big ideas in the story (theme, character, ambiguities)?
- make predictions consistent with the text?

Below is a Grade 5 student's passionate response to a text read.

Feb. 13, '03. Reading Response

I don't understand why those people have to kill the baby gibbons' mothers because everyone needs a mom. Those people should have realized that without their parents they wouldn't even be there! How would they have felt if their mothers were killed? To do something like that, they must be really cruel. They shouldn't kill the animals' moms just for zoo. Zoos aren't as important as parents. Killing animals is like acting as a murderer.

Transition Words

Words that show sequence:	first	next
after as time passed at the same time at this point before concurrently eventually finally	following that fourth immediately in the meantime in the end later meanwhile	now presently previously second simultaneously soon then within minutes
Words that signal the end: all in all briefly in brief in conclusion	in essence in short in summary to conclude	
Unifying expressions: all together also but furthermore	in addition to in the same way likewise moreover	
Words used in comparing and contrasting: but by comparison except in contrast	nevertheless on the other hand unfortunately	
Words that emphasize: always absolutely certainly definitely emphatically eternally	forever in any event never surely unquestionably without a doubt without question	
Words for examples: for example for instance in another case in this case	in this manner in this way	

Rubric for the Assessment of Response to Literature

Name: _____   Date: _____

	Level One In an age-appropriate way:	Level Two In an age-appropriate way:	Level Three In an age-appropriate way
Retell	response shows little or no awareness of major themes or insight into character motivation demonstrates little or no understanding of the author's message	response shows some awareness of major themes and insight into character motivation demonstrates some understanding of the author's message	response shows strong awareness of major themes and insight into character motivation demonstrates a clear and insightful understanding of the author's message
Connect	response makes simple connections to personal experience, but does not develop interpretations or draw conclusions	response makes some connections between own ideas, experiences and opinions that help develop conclusions about the text	response makes insightful connections to own ideas, opinions, personal experiences and feelings that help develop conclusions about the text makes connections to other writing, art, or videos
Reflect	response poses simple questions about the story elements that need little or no inference predictions are not based on textual clues or context; they are more of a guess	response poses questions about the big ideas (theme, character, and ambiguities) questions may help to clarify some points of difficulty in the text predictions are consistent with the text	response poses insightful questions that help deepen understanding of the text and develop inferences questions help clarify points of difficulty in the text predictions are consistent with the text and supported by quotations

Retelling a Story in Parts

Name: _____

Title: _____

1.

Words
* _____
* _____
* _____
* _____
* _____
* _____

2.

Words
* _____
* _____
* _____
* _____
* _____
* _____

3.

Words
* _____
* _____
* _____
* _____
* _____
* _____

4.

Words
* _____
* _____
* _____
* _____
* _____
* _____

3

Writing Nonfiction

Anchor Lesson	Skill Focus
Choosing Key Words	Distinguishing important ideas; choosing interesting details to support the main idea
Organizing Your Notes	Organizing and sequencing point-form notes; creating a logical sequence
Using a Semantic Map	Organizing and sequencing point-form notes; creating a logical sequence; connecting ideas
Reading the Pictures	Extending the text with pictures
Outlining with Questions	Distinguishing important ideas and finding supporting details
Where's the Detail?	Building interesting sentences and paragraphs
Developing Text Features in Research Reports • Exploring a nonfiction book • Finding text features	Understanding and applying text features
Developing Voice	Applying techniques that bring writing to life, such as Zoom in!, Make it your own, and Speak
Creating a Magazine, Textbook or Newspaper	Presenting information in a variety of forms

Nonfiction writing is a critical component of a complete writing program. In practice, however, greater emphasis is often given to narrative and personal accounts. Writing is taught in the language arts period, and students are left to figure out how to write informational text on their own. We believe it is time to redress this imbalance as nonfiction has tremendous power to engage students in inquiry and develop their passion for learning about the world and how it works. Many students who are not particularly interested in writing stories or poems will come to life when given the opportunity to research a topic and write a report.

Just as we do with other writing forms, we begin by reading aloud in the genre, drawing students' attention to the form and style of nonfiction. There are many titles in the school library that can form the basis for a thorough exploration of the way in which different writers present information in interesting ways. While stories and novels are read from cover to cover, nonfiction is different. We can "dip into" nonfiction using the location features of the text to discover answers to our questions. This is an enticing way to hook our students onto the delights of the genre.

Nonfiction writing is also the perfect complement to nonfiction reading. Shared or guided reading lessons are the perfect place for teachers to draw attention to organizational features of nonfiction text, such as the table of contents, index and glossary. When students are engaged in reading factual accounts on such topics as animals, space, or natural phenomena, they note boldface words and the details captured in diagrams and illustrations. The organizational framework of informational texts becomes clearer to students when they are asked to reproduce these forms in their own writing. However, text features need to be taught explicitly if we want students to incorporate these features into their own writing. Our instruction includes making the reading–writing connection transparent.

Supporting Purpose through Text Features

Nonfiction writing has a variety of purposes. It may inform us about something or retell information. It may describe or offer an explanation of a phenomenon. It may tell us how to do something: how to follow a procedure or a set of directions. It may also attempt to persuade us of a point of view. To achieve these purposes, the writing can take a number of different forms. Scientific reports, nonfiction narratives, letters, recipes, rules, directions, reviews, debates, advertisements, journals, autobiographies and biographies are among the many ways we can choose to present information. Our focus in the anchor lessons is on gathering information and presenting it in effective ways.

Various devices are used to make informational text clearer, more explicit and more informative than words alone. We use nonfiction material to directly teach the text features that can help the reader locate specific information. Common features are outlined below.

- A **table of contents** guides the reader to major book parts, such as chapters, and includes page references.
- An **index** lists topics alphabetically and references the pages on which these can be located.
- A **glossary** lists important vocabulary and offers definitions and perhaps a phonetic pronunciation guide.
- **Headings** and **subheadings** are inserted into a text to break it into logical units. They direct the reader's attention to the content of a paragraph or section of text, highlighting major ideas.
- **Sidebars** offer information that supplements the main ideas on that page.
- A **bibliography** cites references to published texts that have been quoted or referred to in the text.
- An **appendix** contains relevant material that supports the main text, such as further examples, charts, and pictures.
- Bolded and italicized fonts signal important words and help readers find definitions.
- Charts, maps, graphs, diagrams, captions and pictures provide specific information, often supplementing or illustrating the text.
- Pronunciation guides use phonetics to show how unusual or challenging words sound.
- Key words, such as "therefore" and "in conclusion," signal important information. They warn the reader to pay attention.
- Opening sentences in paragraphs introduce paragraph content and concluding sentences often summarize it.

Understanding Text Structures

The way that informational text is organized is also important. The particular ways of organizing text are referred to as *text structure*. Students can use their knowledge of organizational patterns to help comprehend what they are reading and help construct their own reports. Informational text is generally organized in one of the following ways:

- **temporal sequence** or **chronology**, for example, when describing events in history such as a military campaign or voyage of exploration
- **cause and effect**, when one event or concept has caused another to come into being. Example: "A spark from a campfire may cause a forest fire."
- **problem and solution**, when a problem is described together with its solution. Example: "The logging of old growth forests leads to the loss of habitat for forest creatures. Environmental groups have been formed to campaign against such forest practices."
- **question** and **answer**, when a question is posed and then answered. Example: "Why does an owl spit out a pellet? It discards the bones and other indigestible parts of its prey."

- **compare and contrast**, when you look at similarities and differences between two things. Example: Comparing the attributes of two people showing how they are alike, and contrasting them, showing how they are different.
- **description or enumeration**, which lists attributes and information about a topic, person or event. Example: "The owl has sharp talons for catching and holding its prey. It has a sharp, curved beak for tearing the prey apart."

Gathering, Organizing and Presenting Information

How many parents have had their sons and daughters come home from school assigned to write a research report only to find that their children have none of the prerequisite skills to fulfill the assignment independently and successfully? Often, students are unsure about note-taking and uncertain about developing their notes into paragraphs. Typically, they are unable to synthesize information adequately. They also need to have options for presenting their finished work as a published piece.

The first group of lessons in this chapter scaffold the process of gathering information before writing. Knowing how to take notes from nonfiction text is an important subskill in developing a research report. Researchers take notes so that they can remember ideas and details to include in reports. Many students do not understand how to take notes nor what is important to note while gathering information for a research report. Frequently, students choose too much information; other simply copy from the text. Teachers need to encourage students to write in single words or short phrases, use their own language, and record only important ideas. Anchor lessons will help students select important information, develop their ability to evaluate ideas, develop their understanding of the concept and importance of note-taking, help them remember important details and ideas, and help them move towards using their own words.

The balance of the chapter focuses on lessons that will help students put information together and explore a few unusual ideas for publishing their texts. Students enjoy the creative challenge of transferring their notes into original formats for sharing with others. The features of magazines, newspapers, and textbooks offer a starting point for publishing.

Nonfiction offers unique challenges for the writer and the writing teacher. The anchor lessons in this chapter are intended to scaffold student and teacher understanding of the subskills involved in report writing. Nonfiction writing can be tremendously satisfying for young writers when they have the prerequisite skills. In the words of one student, "I learn how to write *and* I learn about the world at the same time!"

Writing Profile for Nonfiction

Dimensions of Writing	Undeveloped 1	2-3-4	Fully Developed 5
	At a Glance: The report is brief and hard to understand with loosely connected ideas.		At a Glance: The report is focused, expressive, and clear in intent; it effectively accomplishes the purpose.
Engagement with the Topic • Meaning • Ideas • Details	Report may be unclear or unfocused and is difficult to follow. Purpose is vague. Information may be copied or inaccurate. Details are irrelevant.		Report is focused and clearly directed towards the purpose. Information is accurate and complete. Details support the main ideas and are used with intent to inform and clarify.
Vividness and Language Use • Energy • Passion • Voice • Word Choice • Variety • Expressiveness • Originality • Creativity	Writing lacks energy and evidence of personal engagement with the topic. Voice of the writer is unclear. Language is simple. Technical terminology may be absent or inaccurate.		Language is clear and precise using accurate terminology when appropriate. Ideas are presented with voice and style. Words are chosen for effect. Technical terminology is used accurately and with effect.
Organization and Structure • Sequence • Clarity • Focus • Cohesion	Writing may lack a clear introduction to the topic or conclusion. Report has simple repetitive sentence patterns or poorly constructed sentences. Text features (headings, diagrams, graphics, etc.) are absent or used inappropriately.		Report begins with an arresting lead, flows smoothly, and ends with an effective summation of the information. Writing is cohesive and shows clear logical sequence and paragraphing. Text features (headings, diagrams, graphics, etc.) are used effectively.
Conventions • Spelling • Punctuation • Grammar	Frequent errors in sentence structure, spelling, punctuation and grammar make the writing difficult to understand. Presentation is lacking care.		Basic spelling, punctuation and grammar are correct. Presentation of writing, graphics and illustrations shows care. Special features make the report interesting to the reader.

Choosing Key Words

Why teach this anchor lesson?

- To help students distinguish between important information and supporting detail
- To develop awareness of vocabulary
- To develop the ability to write a focused paragraph

How to do it

1. Select a piece of short text containing information on one topic only. This passage should be at the students' independent reading level. Copy the passage onto an overhead transparency.
2. Read the passage together with the class. Read it again, asking students to put the information in two columns:

Important Information	Interesting Details

It is important to choose an "easy" piece of text because students are learning new information and a new skill at the same time.

3. Work through the short passage with students pausing to "think aloud" about which parts provide important ideas and which ones merely provide interesting details. Often there are more interesting details than important ideas. Deciding what constitutes the main point of a paragraph is part of the skill of analysing a text. There may be debate and students must justify their choices.
4. Students transfer their list of important information onto a key word recording sheet (see BLM 3.1). They then develop their key words into paragraphs and illustrate their topic with a detailed labelled drawing that teaches something extra.
5. Students can save some "interesting details" to include as opening sentences or to illustrate in their "teaching pictures" that extend the text.

Remember the writing anchor: Find the keys.

Student Reflection

- How could you tell the difference between an important fact and an interesting detail?
- How were you able to paraphrase or limit the use of the author's words?

Evaluation

To what extent was the student able to
- select important information?
- choose vocabulary that signalled the main ideas?
- develop key words into a paragraph?

Key Words
fins
lateral line
*stremline body
gills
scales and mucus
eyes
nostrals

Salmon
By: Anna

A salmon has a strem line body. The stremline body helps the salmon to glide esuly through the water. The body is covered in scales. The scales are covered in mucus to prtect it fron Idiseaseses and help it slide though the water. Each fin on the salmons body has a special job. The dorsal fin keeps the salmon balenced. The pelvic fins and pectoral fins are used for turning, backing up and stopir.

Anna   Gr. 2

Why teach this anchor lesson?

- To provide a scaffold for student note-taking
- To help students organize their notes into logical units for paragraph development

How to do it

1. Provide grid paper for note-taking. A grid paper can simply be a piece of paper folded into boxes and numbered with a heading for the topic.
2. Suggest to students that they limit themselves to one topic per grid. For example, if researching an animal, all the grid notes on appearance will go on one page, and all the grid notes on habitat will go on another. When students have multiple sources and multiple topics on mixed grids, organizing them can be overwhelming.
3. Students take their complete grid notes and cut them up. They then sort their notes by subtopics. For example, if the grid notes are about appearance, they might sort them according to physical size, coloration, and special features. Blackline Master 3.2 shows one way to organize notes.
4. Students then paste the key words on a master sheet approximating the order that they could be used in their paragraphs. See Jana's work below.

It may be helpful for students to write about each topic as they go rather than have the overwhelming task of writing the whole thing once all the notes are collected.

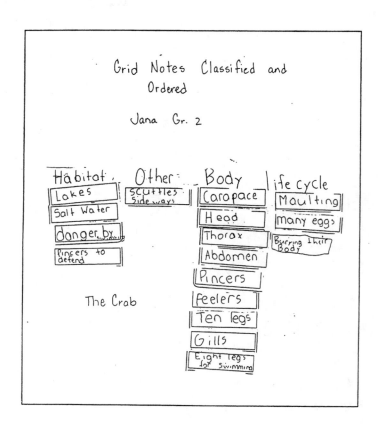

In the first sample, you can see how Nathan moved from point-form notes under certain headings to paragraphs.

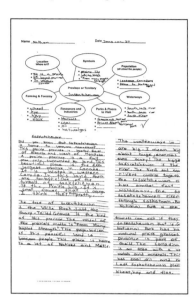

Connor's notes (Grade 4) provide an example of information listed under major headings.

Alternatives: Provide prepared graphic organizers that have predetermined headings depending on the topic. For example, if students are researching Canadian provinces, the headings would likely include Population, Location, Resources and Industries, and Parks. The graphic organizers can be lists, boxes or webs. Students may benefit from the scaffolding.

> Remember the writing anchor: Put ideas in sequence.

Student Reflection

- How does using the grid paper or organizer help you with your note-taking?
- How do the notes help you to draft your paragraphs?

Evaluation

To what extent was the student able to
– sort information under headings?
– transfer notes into organized paragraphs?

Name _____ Connor _____   Subject ___ artic Fox ___

No. ☐ Heading Appearence +
How Big am I ?   Size

No. ☐ Heading Habita
Get out of my house

1. The Artic Fox is 65-85 cm long and weighs 2.5-50 kilograms the (hightris 25 cr.
   ° z weighs 2.5 to 9.0 kg
   ° 115 cm in length
2. Smallest wild canid in Canada.
4. Size of a large demestic cat.
3. Tail is long and brush.
5. making up between 30 and 35% total length.
7. In Canada blue foxes seldom make up more than 5% of animals.
6. In Greenland the proportion of blue foxes may reach fifty %.

1. found Europe, Asia, North America, Greenland, ice land, Canada, Alaska, Russia, Scandinavia and Various Islands also England and Norway
3. live in dens, burrows usual by a cliff or a hill.
2. Dens usually 6-12 fe underground.
5. Near Arctic ocean.
4. pups are born in dens, drained soils of low rise and cutbank.

Using a Semantic Map

Why teach this anchor lesson?

- To provide another structure for organizing notes
- To encourage the connection of ideas and vocabulary

How to do it

1. Prior to reading, choose key words or concepts from the text to be read. For example, if the topic is an animal, the key concepts might be appearance, habitat, food, enemies, habits, protection, and types. If the topic is a country, the key headings would likely include Location, Climate, Religion and Resources.
2. Together, the teacher and students brainstorm their understandings about these concepts and list them as key words in a map or web format. Blackline Master 3.3 provides an outline.
3. Students or the teacher read the reference text, pausing to add information and making corrections to the semantic map. After reading, review with the class to see that all the information they have on their semantic maps is accurate. Cross out any inaccurate ideas that may have been contributed before reading.
4. Students then use the semantic map to organize their paragraphs and complete their reports. As students become familiar with how a semantic map works, they can use it with increasing independence to organize their writing.

> Remember the writing anchor: Find the keys.

Student Reflection

- How did the semantic map help you learn today?
- What are the steps we followed in writing our nonfiction report?
- What will you remember to do when you are working independently on a project of your own?

Evaluation

To what extent was the student able to
- collect specific information about a topic to create a set of key words and phrases?
- develop key words into sentences and paragraphs?
- apply semantic map skill independently?

This example shows the combined expertise of a class prior to reading about rabbits. The words that are crossed out indicate those concepts that were corrected after reading.

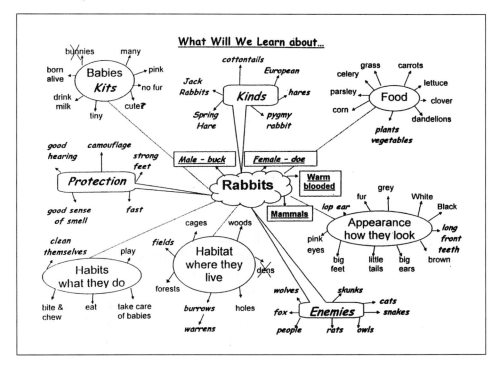

The web on insects shows connections clearly. For example, Body Parts lead to Head leads to large eyes.

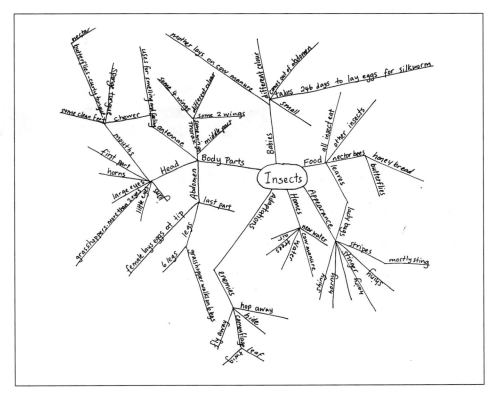

Reading the Pictures

Why teach this anchor lesson?

- To help students learn the importance of reading the pictures, diagrams and illustrations in nonfiction text for more information (These diagrams and illustrations extend the text and inform the reader.)
- To help students understand that they should illustrate their own nonfiction writing in ways that inform the reader

How to do it

Special instructions: Have enlarged photocopies of an informative illustration on the topic of study and sticky notes at hand.

1. Ask students to draw a picture of the subject they are studying before looking at the photograph.
2. Explain to students that authors use pictures in nonfiction texts to *teach* us more about the topic. We can learn a lot of information if we learn to read the pictures.
3. Give out the photocopies and guide students in studying the illustration to see what they can learn. Direct them to look at labels that point out details, if there are any. Ask questions about the parts of the illustration. What is the purpose of that part? Do they know what all the parts are called? Have them use sticky notes to record their observations and stick them on their photocopies. (Students stick the notes in their research notebooks on the appropriate topic page.)
4. Ask students to return to their previous drawings and modify them so that the drawings are not only attractive, but also *teach* about the subject.
5. Apply this technique to the students' independent reading and research. Focus students' attention on "reading the pictures" as they do their researching. Ask them to make their pictures carefully so that they *teach* about the subject. The emphasis is not on an artistic rendition, but on an accurate diagram that conveys information.

Remember the writing anchor: Where's the detail?

Student Reflection

Students may do a "caption match" where they have pictures and captions to pair up. This activity helps teach the importance of reading pictures and could be used as a pre-reading activity to scaffold comprehension.

- How did looking at the pictures help you today?
- What will you remember to do when you make the illustrations for your research report?

Evaluation

To what extent was the student able to
- extract information from an illustration?
- develop illustrations to inform the reader?
- apply this skill independently?

These diagrams show how attention to detail in a student's drawing can add information to a report that goes beyond the words.

Sea urchin
Rightside-up
— The spikes protects the sea urchin from predators.

Sea urchin
Underneath
Sea urchins are related to sea stars because of the shape.

The five shapes surrounding it's mouth are it's teeth.

The Mouth is on the bottom of the sea urchin.

Laura
Gr. 2

Owl Facts   Gloria Gr.2

Owl eats Mice
Owl eats Fish
Owl eats Worm
Owl eats Bug
Owl eats Snake
Owl eats Small Bird
Owl

Key Words
✱fur ✓
✱Alone ✓
✱Whole ✓
✱bones ✓
Prey ✓
✱Pellets ✓
Digests ✓
Coughs up ✓

Outlining with Questions

Why teach this anchor lesson?

- To help young researchers anticipate questions a reader may have about a topic and focus their inquiry on finding the answers

How to do it

1. Model and think aloud to show students the process of anticipating questions. For example: "I noticed a newspaper article about a prize-winning pumpkin. This pumpkin weighed 250 kg! I have some questions about these pumpkins and I think people who read my report will have some questions too. I am going to make a list of questions my readers will want answered in my work." Write Who? What? When? Where? Why? How? and generate questions much like the following with the class:

   1. Where are giant pumpkins grown?
   2. Do giant pumpkins come from special seeds or can any pumpkin become a giant?
   3. How big is the biggest pumpkin ever grown?
   4. Where do giant pumpkins grow?
   5. What do they do with the giant pumpkins?
   6. Are there contests to see which is the biggest pumpkin?
   7. Where are the contests held?
   8. What do pumpkins need to grow really big?
   9. Can anyone produce huge pumpkins?

2. Continue by saying something like this: "Now I need to organize my questions in order by thinking about what the reader will need to know about first, second and so on. I think I'll catch the reader's attention by putting #3, about the biggest pumpkin ever grown, first so they will be amazed by how big giant pumpkins really are. Then it makes sense to tell the reader where they grow, #4, and then #2, about the seeds. After that, I'll write about #8, what giant pumpkins need to grow big, and I'll go on to the information about contests for giant pumpkins, #6 and 7. From there I will write about what they do with the giant pumpkins, #5. I'll close with #9 and a challenge to kids to try to grow a giant pumpkin of their own."

3. Students sit in talking pairs and discuss Who? What? When? Where? Why? How? questions for their topic.

4. Students record their questions on separate strips of paper and, with partners, move them into a logical order.

> Remember the writing anchors: Find the keys. Put ideas in sequence.

Student Reflection

· How did thinking of questions help you to make an outline for your research?
· What will you remember to do when you are working on an independent research project?

Evaluation

To what extent was the student able to
– generate questions to focus their inquiry?
– develop a logical sequence?
– apply this skill independently?

In this sample, Jennifer, a Grade 7 student, has organized her snail research under the topics generated by her questions.

Jennifer   April 10, 2003

Snails

1. Where do snails live?
   · Cool, shady, moist places
   · Under logs.
   · Old boards, in piles of dead leaves.

2. What is the snails appearance?
   · Flat, coiled shell.
   · Look like cones
   · Tiny.

3. What are the contents inside the snails shell?
   · Tentacles.
   · A tiny breathing pore.
   · The snails lungs.

4. How do snails move?
   · One foot.
   · Gastropod
   · Stomach foot.

Jennifer   April 10, 2003

Snails cont

5. What do snails eat?
   · Plants
   · Flowers, roots
   · Fruits, vegtables.

6. Where do snails go in dry weather?
   · Body functions slow down
   · Estivation.
   · Devises Moisture.

7. Where do baby snails come from?
   · Hermaphrodites.
   · Fertalizes the eggs.
   · Lays up to 50 eggs.

8. Can snails live underwater?
   · Relatives in oceans.
   · Gills.
   · Others feed on shellfish.

Where's the Detail?

Why teach this anchor lesson?

· To help students organize their notes into sentences and paragraphs
· To assist them in learning how to create compound sentences with relevant details

How to do it

Session 1: Building sentences

1. Explain that the key words and phrases recorded on a semantic map or in point-form notes do not make sense by themselves. In order to make a complete sentence, more words will have to be added.
2. Using a semantic map that the class has created, take a key word and demonstrate how to build it into a sentence. For example, using the ideas collected on the semantic map about rabbits, we see that a rabbit's food includes a variety of plants and vegetables. A sentence about food might say, "Rabbits eat plants and vegetables, including grass, dandelions, clover, parsley, lettuce and carrots."
3. Together, teacher and students build sentences using key words.
4. Students choose a section of key words from the class web previously created and develop them on sentences strips.
5. Students hand in their sentence strips. These are then shared among small groups. The students work together to combine sentences. For example, students might work with these sentences: Owls have sharp talons. Owls hold their prey with their talons. Students could combine them into "Owls have sharp talons with which they hold their prey."
6. Using the sentence strips, students create combined sentences that are more detailed.

Session 2: Building paragraphs

1. Prepare on strips up to eight sentences that all refer to the same topic. One of them should be an umbrella sentence that introduces a topic. Don't group or order them yet, but display them in random order in a pocket chart if you have one; alternatively, using masking tape, tape the sentence strips to a white board or chalkboard.
2. Read the sentences and then ask the students to pick the one they think is the best topic sentence for the paragraph. Have them suggest ways of ordering the sentences such that similar ideas are grouped together. Number the sentences and then write them in paragraph form, modelling how to combine sentences and how to use pronouns appropriately. For example, if the topic of the report is rabbits, the word "rabbits" may be replaced with "They."
3. Following this whole-class activity, distribute a prepared set of sentences on another topic on a worksheet.
4. Students cut up the sentences and then organize them by selecting a topic sentence and grouping similar ideas together. They then write a good copy of this paragraph.

Student Reflection

- How did having the sentences prepared for you help you to compose an interesting and logical paragraph?
- What did you learn about combining short choppy sentences to make longer, more interesting ones?

Evaluation

To what extent was the student able to
– write paragraphs that have a logical structure?
– combine ideas to create interesting sentences?

Developing Text Features in Research Reports

Why teach this anchor lesson?

- To build reading and writing skills by giving students insight into the organization and construction of nonfiction texts
- To teach students how to use particular features of nonfiction text that make it possible to locate specific information without reading the whole book cover to cover
- Grades 2–3 students will use a few boldface words and develop a simple table of contents and a glossary; Grades 4–7 students will include the boldface words, a table of contents and glossary, a bibliography and an index.

How to do it

Session 1: Exploring a nonfiction book

1. A demonstration of how the teacher might work with a nonfiction book appears below.

   TEACHER: Let's examine some information books to see what features make them different from story books. Nonfiction books are organized so that the reader can dip in and find the information they are looking for without reading the whole book. If you know how a book is organized, you can find the information easily. Here I have a book about bats. Let's start by generating some questions and see if we can locate the answers. What questions do you have about bats?

   STUDENT: Where do bats live?

   TEACHER: Let's see if we can use the features of the book to answer that question. Let's look first in the table of contents. I'll read you the chapter headings. Listen to see if you hear anything about bats' habitat.

   Together the teacher and students agree on the appropriate section and refer to the pages listed. The teacher draws the students' attention to the helpfulness of the table of contents. The lesson continues:

   STUDENT: Are there vampire bats?

   TEACHER: Did you hear about vampire bats in the table of contents? There's another feature in a nonfiction book called the index. Let's see if it is mentioned there.

   And so forth.

Session 2: Finding text features

1. Review features of nonfiction text introduced the previous day and develop a chart for reference. (See BLM 3.4.)
2. Put students into working pairs and give each partnership two or three nonfiction texts that contain excellent examples of the features of nonfiction texts.
3. Using Blackline Master 3.5, students locate the features of the text and record the usefulness of each.

4. Partners select a text and develop several questions about the contents. They record their questions on Blackline Master 3.6.
5. Students use the nonfiction features to locate the answers to their questions and record them on their worksheet.

> Remember the writing anchors: Make it your own! Find the keys. Where's the detail? Use text features.

Student Reflection

- What are some of the features of nonfiction texts that make it easy to locate information?
- Which features will you include when you write your report?

Evaluation

To what extent was the student able to
– locate information using text features?
– use text features in the writing of a report?

Anthony's report on polar bears shows just how many features of nonfiction text he has learned. He opens his introduction with a question posed directly to the reader and continues by answering the question. His report includes a table of contents, dedication, labelled diagram and glossary.

In The World Of Polar Bears

By Anthony

Table Of Contents

Dedication

I dedicate this book to all the Polar Bears in world. (No Polar Bears were hurt in the making of book).

Introduction

Which animal is the king of all beasts? I guessed Lion, you're right. But in the Arctic, the Polar Bear. The Inuit have lived with Pola years. They call them Ice King. They say tha Polar Bears help them hunt. When hunting, Po dig holes in the ground to catch seals. When the Inuit use those holes to catch fish.

If you want to learn more about the Pola turn the page. Get ready for the read of your

Does This Make Me Look Fat?

Picture nine centimetres of fat. That's what the Polar Bear has around its body. The fat is from what it eats but it's not that kind. It's blubber, a skin that insulates the body heat.

Do you know where the Polar Bear gets its heat? Warmth comes from its black inner fur. The fur covers the whole body. The body is usually two to three centimetres long. The tail is eight to thirteen centimetres. The sensitive ears are only nine centimetres. Last, but not least, the oar-like feet are a staggering thirty-three centimetres long! That's longer than a ruler!

Look At What I Can Do!

If you were cold and alone on the Arctic, go over to a Polar Bear and you'll get instant warmth! Be careful! Don't go too close or else it'll slash you with its five sharp three-inch claws.

If the Polar Bear starts to come your way, walk away slowly. Never try to run away and never try to swim! Polar Bears can run sixty kilometres per hour. That's as fast as the cars on the street! They also never slip because on the bottom of their foot is a pad of papillae. Papillae is a pad of skin that puts friction in between the foot and the ground. Don't try swimming either because they can swim over forty kilometres per hour. What's more they have large oar-like feet that helps them propel forward. They will not tire out because they have nine centimetres of blubber to keep them warm.

We Need A Fireplace!

Polar Bears don't live in very many places, only in the Arctic and Alaska. Sometimes they live in Labrador. The home range of one female and one male can be anywhere from fifty thousand to sixty thousand square kilometres. That's just a small one! Large home ranges are over three hundred thousand square kilometres. That's about two Canadian provinces.

Ears To Listen From Far Distances.

Sensitive Nose For Finding Food

Large Legs And Muscle- Help It Run Fast

Sharp Teeth For Biting Through Prey

Large Feet For Running Or For Swimming

Five Sharp Claws For Tearing Apart Prey

Anthony

Bon Apetit

You wouldn't want to be this bear's chef! Polar Bears have to eat at least two kilograms of fat a day to survive. Polar Bears will eat almost anything they find. Some things they eat are seals, plants, berries, reindeer, small rodents, sea birds, ducks, fish, eggs, human garbage, young walruses and even beluga whales. When Polar Bears eat any animal with fat, they will eat the animals fat first. Then the Polar Bear will devour the meat. The most surprising thing is that Polar Bears never drink water. The way it gets liquid is through its food.

Developing Voice

What is "voice" anyway? *In What a Writer Needs*, Ralph Fletcher says: "When I talk about voice, I mean written words that carry with them the sense that someone has actually written them. Not a committee, not a computer, but a single human being. Writing with voice has the same quirky cadence that makes human speech so impossible to resist listening to" (p. 68). Vibrant nonfiction writing requires synthesis of the information with existing knowledge and inclusion of a personal response.

Refer students to the writing anchors Zoom in! Speak!, Make it your own! and Find a hook, for example, to remind them of the features of vivid writing that they have already explored.

Why teach this anchor lesson?

- To teach students to let their voice be heard in nonfiction writing, rather than writing a stiff and stilted list of facts. Not: "Beavers have _____. Beavers eat _____. Beavers live _____."

How to do it

Version 1: Using the student sample "I'm Looking Good" by Alanna (Grade 4)

I'm Looking Good

Can you look around your mouth and count the lines there are to tell you how old you are? I know for a fact that you can't, but puffins can. If you look at their beaks and count the grooves, they will have 1 groove when the puffin is two years of age. One and a half when it is three years old, and it will have 2 grooves when — you guessed it — it's four years of age.

So now I have you on track about the bill. I'm going to tell you what colour it is. The outer portion of the beak is bright red, as red as maple tree leaves that have fallen to the ground. The beak's inner portion is bright blue, as bright as the sky on a clear day, in the summer. The corners of the bill are as bright as a lemon. That's a very multi-coloured beak! But their bill is not always that colourful. In fact, their beak is grey until they are 4 years old and every winter their bill is dull yellow, like a worn out old yellow jacket. But their bill is blue, yellow, and red in the summer. Surprisingly, the puffin has a spine on the top, inside of the beak. Also in their mouth is yellow skin.

Do you have dark brown or hazel eyes? Then YOU have something in common with puffins. Puffins have hard scaly areas below and above their eyes, that are a pretty bright blue. They also have bright red scaly areas around the eyes. So you don't have something in common with them.

The puffin's body is somewhat like a snowman, just not as fat! They have a round body and head. Puffins also has white on it's stomach, but it has black on it's back. The puffin is a short, stocky, and sturdy sea bird.

1. Ask the students to create a web showing all the ways in which the student writer used her own voice. Do this as a class, recording the ideas on the web and on the blackboard. As the ideas emerge, make sure that students copy them onto their own personal webs, which will be used for future reference.
2. Next, look at the web on voice. Some of the features in this piece include show, not tell, speaking directly to the reader, making comparisons, using expressive language, sharing personal opinions and a personal point of view, and asking questions that are immediately answered.
3. Once the features of writing with voice have been identified, relate these to the anchor lessons already taught and remind students of the anchors. Ask the students to take a paragraph from their own report writing and revise it, adding some features of personal voice.
4. Have students share with a partner, discussing how voice was added.

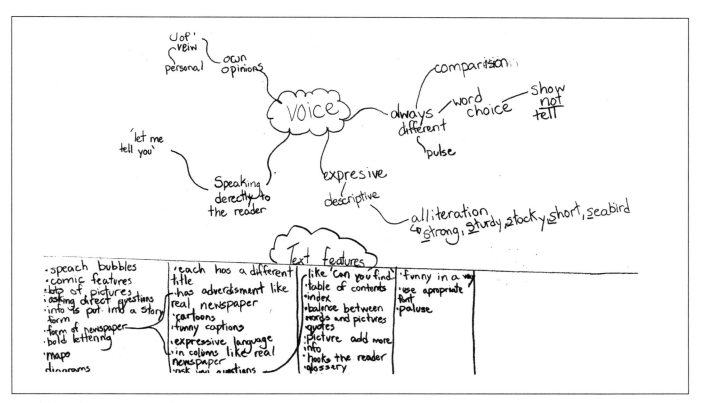

In the handwritten concept map:

voice
- U of view / personal — own opinions
- comparison
- always different — word choice — show not tell
- pulse
- 'let me tell you'
- Speaking derectly to the reader
- expresive / descriptive
- alliteration — strong, sturdy, stocky, short, seabird

Text features

• speach bubbles • comic features • lotp of pictures • asking direct questions • info is put into a story form • form of newspaper • bold lettering • maps • diagrams	• each has a different title • has advertisment like real newspaper • cartoons • funny captions • expressive language • in colums like real newspaper • ask you questions	• like 'can you find' • table of contents • index • balance between words and pictures • quotes • picture add more info • hooks the reader • glossary	• funny in a way • use apropriate font • pause

In this sample the Grade 5 student uses expressive vocabulary to describe how the Spartan army took children to train for war.

In this piece the writer speaks directly to the reader. "Imagine you are a dragon . . ." The piece comes to life with this conversational style.

Grade 5 ~ Writing with voice

expand

In the Kingdom of Sparta When you are seven years of age the soldiers of Sparta will come and pry you from your familie's arms and take you to train for war. The one comfort you have is the chance at glory in your enemies demise

---

Dragons

Imagine (you are) you're a Dragon and you need a home, but where? Your a warm blooded creature so any place is fine. You first think maybe Europe. Um...that may not be the best of chocies. Europians belive your a trecheras beast that will eat them. You are all the evil fought by them. Do you want that? Didn't think so. I would suggest a contry like China or Japan. There you are considered friendly and ensure good luck and wealth. Chinepse. even dress up like you on New Years. They belive you pervent evil spirits from spoilir there fun and laughter Certin dragons have the power to controll rain fall needed every year for harvest, and that 'certin dagon' could be you!

Gr. 5 student
June 2004
Writing with voice

Version 2: Using published nonfiction

1. Use excellent examples of nonfiction writing and contrast that writing with encyclopedic writing. Draw attention to the differences. Look at the ways in which writers made their writing interesting to catch the attention of the reader.

Examples of voice in nonfiction text:

> Clouds are made of droplets of water. Water is heavier than air. So you're quite right: the clouds ought to drop out of the sky! And yet they don't. (Russell Stannard as cited in *Wolves, Eyes, and Stormy Skies*, p. 105)

> Inside the beehive, the honeybees are building an amazing structure called *a honeycomb*. It is made up of countless six-sided cells. Stored in many of these wax cells is the food that bees and people love to eat . . . honey! (Gail Gibbons, *The Honey Makers*)

> The crowd leans over expectantly. A few hang back. They have heard the stories about mummy unwappings — the dead insects that fall to the floor as the bandages are removed, the limbs, suddenly released from their bindings, that slowly rise into the air, as if alive. (Shelley Tanaka, *Secrets of the Mummies*, p. 4)

2. This activity can also include listing text features that are designed to add interest to the text. Students can go on a treasure hunt with a variety of nonfiction books and articles, deconstructing the way in which the writing was put together. On a class list or web, record all the ways in which the writers and illustrators made the information interesting to the reader.

> Remember the writing anchors: Make it your own! Use text features.

Student Reflection

- What can authors do to speak with "voice" in their writing?
- Where have you used your writer's voice?
- What will you remember to do when you are writing nonfiction in the Writing Workshop?

Evaluation

To what extent was the student able to
– reveal his or her voice in the writing?

Creating a Magazine, Textbook or Newspaper

Why teach this anchor lesson?

- To help students understand the features of textbooks, newspapers or magazines in order to use them effectively as information resources
- To provide an opportunity for students to demonstrate their understanding of text features in nonfiction
- To provide an opportunity for students to demonstrate their ability to synthesize information and present it in a new form
- To challenge students with the novelty of writing in a new form

This activity is best done toward the end of a unit of study. Since it requires much information synthesis, students should already have extensive background knowledge before tackling it. Students may be overwhelmed if both the content and the format are new to them. Allow two to three weeks for students to complete a magazine, textbook or newspaper.

How to do it

1. Provide opportunities to explore a magazine, a newspaper, and a textbook to discover the features of each. Create a chart with students, listing specific features of the text form. For example, using the Grade 3 social studies book *Our Communities* by Sharon Sterling, students discovered these text features: Information is given in short paragraphs with pictures, captions, and focus questions. Important information is signalled by different colors. There is a "big question" to focus the reader. Boldface words are included in a glossary. The textbook includes a table of contents and an index. In *Chickadee* magazine, information is presented in these forms: as comics, as games, as riddles, in short articles with captions and pictures, as a picture book with a one-sentence story line, as science experiments, as surveys and in the table of contents. In *The Greek News*, life in ancient Greece is chronicled as if in a newspaper of the time. (This book formed the model for the student sample "The Cabot News," which was generated on a computer by a Grade 5 student.)
2. Ask students to generate the second half of the chart, listing the key concepts from the unit of study. Students can then "mix and match" content with format.
3. Ask students to plan their magazine, newspaper or textbook, deciding which content they will use in which format.
4. Provide paper cut to appropriate sizes as students make decisions about how best to convey the information: sidebar strip? caption? labelled diagram? lined paper? plain paper? Older students could cut their own paper.

After a frog study, Richard chose to share what he had learned in a magazine format. His magazine contained the following:

- a title page featuring a snake chasing a frog
- a table of contents
- "Frog's Diet" information with illustrations and captions
- a board game "From Tadpoles to Frogs"
- "Cool Facts" written in a sidebar
- "Frogs and Their Enemies" information with illustrations and captions
- "The Mating Cycle" as nonfiction narrative
- a computer crossword using frog study vocabulary

Remember the writing anchor: Present with pizazz!

Student Reflection

- What features of your project did you enjoy most?
- When you read a textbook, magazine or newspaper next time, what will you remember about the way such texts are organized?
- How do the features of a textbook, magazine or newspaper help you to find the information you need?

Evaluation

To what extent was the student able to
– organize information in new ways to convey what he or she knows?
– apply the text features of a textbook, magazine or newspaper, such as simple charts, webs, or illustrations, to organize or present information?
– demonstrate a willingness to experiment with communication forms to respond to, inform and entertain others?

Excerpts from three student projects follow. "The Cabot Chronicle" is set up as a newspaper, complete with ads, articles and a contest. The project on Fort Langley is set up as a chapter book with pictures and text; and the frog magazine, mentioned earlier, includes a game, illustrations and text.

The Cabot Chronicle

Issue 1 Volume 1   June 1, 1501   *"Everything fit to read about John Cabot"*   Only 3 pence

"Land, Ho!" - explorer excites King with forest, fish finds

Cabot couldn't see golden temples reported by Columbus, but Henry VII impressed by small tools and account of Cabot's initial voyage . . .

By Roxanne King

When John Cabot was a child the Arab countries controlled almost all the land surrounding the Mediterranean Sea

Ships couldn't sail through the Mediterranean without permission Merchants in Venice had the greatest fleet of ships in Europe. They only gave Venetian ships permission to carry all the ivory, spices, silks and gems They traded the cargo for cloth, wood and metal materials the Arab countries needed Venice's merchants could charge as much as they liked for their precious cargo

Other seafaring countries of Europe thought this was unfair so they started searching for other routes to Asia. They wanted their share of the wealth from India, China and Japan John Cabot believed there was a shorter way to Asia

He had already approached King Ferdinand of Spain and King John II of Portugal. His idea was to find a westward route of Asia. Neither king was willing to give money for such a voyage

After much persuasion by Cabot, Spain's Queen Isabella agreed to finance his 1492 expedition. Bristol's most important merchants agreed to supply him with a fleet of ships. All he needed now was permission from the King of England. Without his permission and a royal charter, Cabot couldn't claim any discoveries in the name of England It would be free for the taking by any European country

Cabot asked King Henry VII (also known as "The Penny Pincher") for the charter Henry quickly gave Cabot the charter, enabling him to discover new lands and sources of trade

On May 2, 1497, John Cabot set sail on the Matthew with a crew of 18 men

He was surprised he didn't see any golden temples along the beach Columbus had spoken about Cabot strained his eyes to see the golden domes and jewelled palaces of the East. He only saw a large thick for-

Continued on page 3

PEOPLE

The curious stowaway

By Roxanne King

Explorer John Cabot managed to sneak into Mecca without getting caught!

John Cabot of Bristol, England has always been curious about the valuable cargo from the Middle East and where exactly it came from.

To satisfy his curiosity, Cabot quietly left his ship while it was in a harbor in Alexandria. He secretly traveled over land to Mecca

Outsiders are not allowed into this holy land of the Arab world Cabot wore a disguise so he was freely able to see the famous city for himself. He had to keep his face covered carefully

Continued on page 2

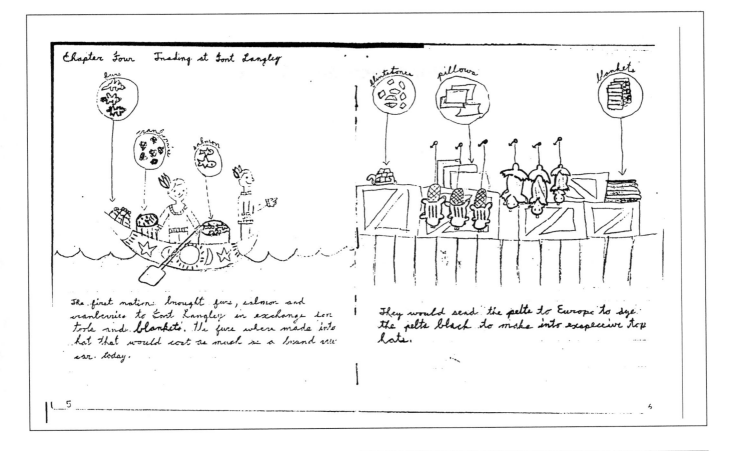

The first nation: brought furs, salmon and cranberries to Fort Langley in exchange for tools and blankets. The furs where made into hat that would cost as much as a brand new car today.

They would send the pelts to Europe to dye the pelts black to make into expensive top hats.

5

6

TADPOLES TO FROGS

This frog has just found dinner. But a prediter is just nearby.

What do frogs eat? Do you belive that frogs eat other frogs? Read this and you'll find out. Frogs eat insects, worms, small rodents, and even other frogs! When a frog is waiting for dinner to come, it sits absolutely still. When it spoted an insect close enough had to reach, it flicks out its tongue, grabs the insect, and throws it down its throw.

A two players game. Place game pieces on the start. Roll dice and move that many spaces. Follow instructions printed on space.

2

Key Word Recording Sheet

Name: _____ Date: _____

Key Words

_____

_____

_____

_____

_____

_____

_____

Note-taking Diagram

Name: _____   Date: _____

Main Topic [   ]

Introduction: Key Words

- _____
- _____
- _____

Subtopics:

| 1. | 2. | 3. | 4. |

Key words

- _____
- _____
- _____
- _____
- _____
- _____
- _____
- _____

Key words

- _____
- _____
- _____
- _____
- _____
- _____
- _____
- _____

Key words

- _____
- _____
- _____
- _____
- _____
- _____
- _____

Key words

- _____
- _____
- _____
- _____
- _____
- _____
- _____

Conclusion:
_____
_____
_____
_____
_____
_____

The Semantic Map

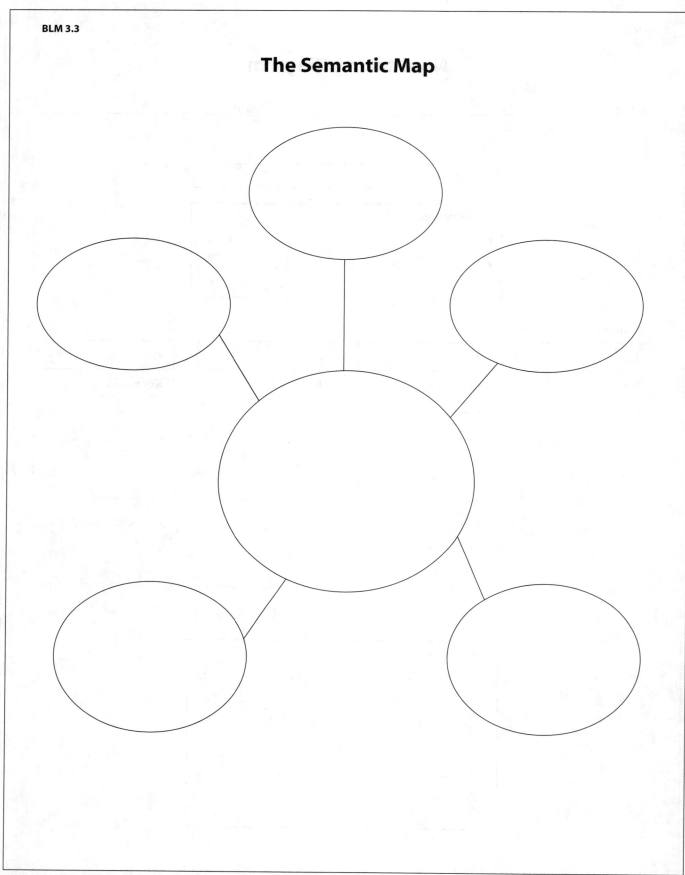

Text Features 1

Nonfiction text may have

- a table of contents
- chapter headings
- section headings
- reading tips
- focus questions to get you thinking as you read
- boldface words
- italicized words
- definitions
    - in brackets
    - in context
    - in glossary
- captions
- sidebars
- a glossary
- an index
- a bibliography

Text Features 2

Text Feature	What I found there	Why this feature is useful
Table of Contents		
Boldface Words		
Sidebars		

Text Feature	What I found there	Why this feature is useful
Captions		
Index		
Bibliography		

Text Features 3

Our Question	The Answer	Where Found (name the text feature)
Where do bats go in winter?	Most bats in northern climates migrate to caves and abandoned mines. There they hibernate in colonies. Bats in warm climates do not migrate or hibernate.	Index

4

Writing Poetry

Anchor Lesson	Skill Focus
The Senses in Color • From the generic to the specific • From paint chips to strong images	Using sensory language; developing voice through specific language
Things I Love • Exploring voice • Being specific	Using sensory language; developing voice through specific language
The Five Senses and the Weather • A sensory walk • Choosing images	Using sensory language; developing voice through specific language
Using Poet's Eyes	Developing metaphors and similes
Images in the Environment	Developing metaphors and similes
Poetry Cut-ups: Playing with Words	Choosing words for special effect
More about Metaphors and Similes	Developing metaphors and similes
Repetition Heightens Impact	Choosing words for special effect
The Magic Box	Using sensory language; choosing words or special effect
Show, Don't Tell: Think of a Time • Guided imagery • Reshaping a class poem	Telling the inside and outside experiences; playing with white space and line breaks

Because poems are often shorter in length than other forms of writing, children can select their words and images carefully using their time to craft their work and capture the feelings they want to express. Often, children who struggle with writing can be successful with poetry as they express their ideas with originality.

Before children are set to work composing poems of their own, they need to enjoy the rhyme, rhythm and repetition of poetry read aloud. They will delight in poetic devices such as alliteration and metaphor long before they have words to name them. Through read-alouds and shared reading, students come to understand the poetic form, develop a sense of the range of forms that poetry can take, and cultivate favorite poets. In short, before students write, they need to have fun with the deliciousness of poems.

Savoring the Sounds of Poetry

There are many ways you can help students enjoy poetry, especially when read aloud. When you first read aloud, demonstrate the rhythm and expression, then reread to clarify vocabulary and meaning. The class reads aloud in unison.

Be sure to revisit favorite poems regularly and read them in new ways. Try some of these activities with your students:

- Divide the class in half and alternate lines, stanzas or parts.
- Read the poem aloud as Readers Theatre with individuals, pairs, trios and whole-class opportunities to read.
- Read aloud in a variety of voices, for example, like a wrestler, like a queen.
- Read aloud varying the tempo and the volume.

Teacher Brenda Boylan makes particularly effective use of the strategy of getting students to love poetry before they begin to write it. "Poetry needs time. Every day, my morning starts off with a poem (five minutes). I echo-read the poem (the children repeat each line back to me). This is a great way to involve kids in the reading of poetry, allowing them to hear the rhythm and beat of the poem. I reread the same poem often. Children love to hear their favorites read over and over again. One of the best poetry books to begin this with is Loris Lesynski's *Dirty Dog Boogie*. This collection of poems is both fun and contagious and can be read from September to June.

"Once children begin to enjoy poetry, I reinforce that this is a great genre to explore during writing times. I make poetry a part of my literacy centres by creating a Build-a-Poem centre where a small group of children or individual children can write a poem using my chart stand and special felts. Children love to use their teacher's materials, and allowing them to have a big space to write, such as the chart stand, inspires them to create amazing poetry."

Further the enjoyment of poetry by

- introducing students to the poetry section in the school library

Poetry lends itself to publishing at all grades. It is meant to be enjoyed aloud and shared with others. We keep a photo album — the kind with sticky, transparent pages — in our classroom for students to add their published poems. We also compile class poems into books and encourage students to create their own poetry anthologies in booklet form. All of these are great favorites for reading.

- requiring students to include a poetry anthology in their choices for independent reading
- featuring new poets in read-aloud regularly
- reminding students to mumble-read their poems to themselves as poems are to be enjoyed orally

Encourage students to spend "noisy reading time" enjoying poems together. For this purpose, establish a poetry collection in the classroom that includes published and student-made books, and create collections of poems on charts or in binders.

An Awareness of Poetic Elements

Teachers also have a role to play in helping students to identify poetic elements through direct instruction. Here is a scenario of a teacher discussing the poem "The Wendigo" with a group of students. Depending on students' age and attention, this conversation might take place over a few days.

"Listen to me read this poem by Ogden Nash aloud for you. Then we will look at some of the difficult words and talk about what they mean. See if the words help you to create a picture of the Wendigo in your mind as I read it . . . "

THE WENDIGO

The Wendigo,
The Wendigo!
Its eyes are ice and indigo!
Its blood is rank and yellowish!
Its voice is hoarse and bellowish!
Its tentacles are slithery,
And scummy,
Slimy, Leathery!
Its lips are hungry blubbery,
And smacky,
Sucky,
Rubbery!

The Wendigo,
The Wendigo!
I saw it just a friend ago!
Last night it lurked in Canada;
Tonight on your veranda!
As you are lolling hammockwise
It contemplates you stomachwise.
You loll,
It contemplates,
It lollops.
The rest is merely gulps and gollops.

Source: "The Wendigo" by Ogden Nash from *Creatures, Kings, and Scary Things*, Anthology 3. © by Curtis Publishing Company. Reprinted by permission of Curtis Brown Ltd.

"Ogden Nash has described the Wendigo using his senses. What words help us to see the Wendigo? hear the Wendigo? to know how it would feel? smell? Are there tasting words in this poem?

"Now face a partner nearby and take turns describing the Wendigo you see in your mind. Have a look at the shape of the poem. How is it different from a story shape? Tell your partner how this poem looks compared to a story.

"Poets play with white space to make their poem look interesting on the page. Some lines are long and some are short. Let's look at the pattern of long and short lines in this poem. What do you notice?

"This poem has two stanzas. How does each one begin? What is the topic in the first stanza? What is the topic in the second? Tell your partner your ideas.

"Ogden Nash has also used repetition in this poem. Which lines are repeated? How does this make a better poem?

"I am noticing that some lines have made-up words. Can you find them? You see, poets often play with words. They take a risk and invent language.

"Let's read it again and feel the rhythm of the poem. Let's clap the beat as we say it again with scary, whispery voices.

"Poets often use a device called *alliteration*. That's when words start with the same sounds. Can you find any examples of alliteration in this poem?"

And so forth.

When we teach the poetic form through discussion such as this, students will begin to develop metacognitive awareness of poetic elements. They can begin to generate a list of characteristics with the class. Ask students, "What do you know about poems?" You will get responses such as the following:

- sometimes rhymes, but it doesn't need to
- "plays with words"
- uses words deliberately to create an effect
- has lines instead of sentences
- has stanzas instead of paragraphs
- uses white space effectively
- may have similes, metaphors and alliteration
- often expresses emotion
- has a strong ending

You will note that the Writing Profile for Poetry (see page 97) reflects these elements under the dimensions of Engagement with the Topic, Vividness and Language Use, Organization and Structure, and Conventions in free verse poetry.

The poetry anchor lessons focus on ways to scaffold student understanding of poetry. Like all anchor lessons, they are designed to develop students' internal control over the procedures used to scaffold writing with "in the head" strategies that can be applied in Writing Workshop. We like to use the language of the anchor lesson when we respond to the work or celebrate success at the beginning of the Writing Workshop each day. For example: "You used 'poet's eyes' when you said, 'The shell looks like a pirate's leg.' I get a picture in my mind of just what that shell looks like." Always celebrate success. As we demonstrate for students what is expected and admired, they will continue to craft and polish their writing.

Through the anchor lessons, teachers and students can gain confidence in their ability to take poetry writing to new heights. Teachers come to understand

We discourage children from attempting to rhyme as their poems tend to become banal and commonplace.

Remember that nothing inspires student writing like the work of their classmates. Capitalize on this by reproducing student work on charts or on overheads. Discuss the successful aspects of the work with the class prior to Writing Workshop. Ask the students, "What is powerful in this poem?"

the aspects of poetry that students need to make their writing stronger and students are equipped with tools to shape their writing independently in the Writing Workshop.

Some Ideas for Structuring Poetry Writing

One of the easiest ways to get started with poetry writing is to provide students with a structure, or frame. Below, you will find four simple ideas for structuring a poem. Students enjoy working with these frames, and they provide a scaffold for further explorations.

Make a sandwich: A descriptive list poem

The sandwich form is also used in the lesson plan titled "Things I Love."

The poem begins and ends with the same sentence, phrase or word. Below is a student-written example.

> I like sounds
>   The crisp sound of paper
>   The rustling of corn
>   The roar of a river
>   The jingle of money
> I like sounds

A small group of students can choose a focus and develop poems together on a large chart on the floor. Their poems may be "Our Favorite Sights" or "Our Favorite Sounds."

Provide a frame: The simile frame

Students may need support in structuring their ideas. Offer a frame to begin and end the poem. For example:

What is a _____ like?
          (body of poem)
     Now you know what a _____ is like.

The poem below by a Grade 3 student named Jennifer provides a good model for classroom use.

> What is a snail like?
> A snail is like a trail blazer,
> A graceful skater,
> A snail is like it's made out of glass,
> It's pleased to pass.
> It is like a rock,
> The body glistens, it shines.
> It has a mobile home,
> It is like a fan opening,
> Now you know what a snail is like.

What am I?: The metaphor frame

Students choose a topic and write clues in metaphor form for classmates to guess their identity.

> *What am I?*
> *I am a wrestler in a 4-way match*
> *A football player in a game*
> *I am Zorro in a fight with the king*
> *A gangster with a motorcycle*
> *A blade from a chain saw*
> *I am a rock star with a guitar*
> *I am a fiddler crab.*
>
> *By Jordan*

Create a list poem

Students can work alone or in small groups with large charts on the floor. One option is to begin every line with "Why."

> *Why do hens lay eggs?*
> *Why do camels have bumps?*
> *Why are tears salty?*
> *Why does God have powers?*
> *Why do clocks tell time?*

Etc.

Other Topics for List Poems

- Things I wonder . . .
- If I were in charge of the world . . .
- The best things about_____
- Why I love _____(chocolate, forests, my pet)
- _____ is (summer, ice cream, bubblegum, a leaf)
- Things that make me _____ (happy, sad, curious, angry, scared)
- Ten reasons to _____
- Ten things to do with _____

Writing Profile for Poetry

Dimensions of Writing	Undeveloped 1	2-3-4	Fully Developed 5
	At a Glance: Poem lacks originality; it is clichéd and fails to engage the reader.		At a Glance: The poem engages the reader; it is original and creative.
Engagement with the Topic • Meaning • Ideas • Details	Text may be unclear or illogical. There is little development of ideas. Writing lacks impact.		Poem conveys meaning clearly. Poem is fully developed in an unusual or original way. Writing creates an impact on the reader.
Vividness and Language Use • Energy • Passion • Voice • Word Choice • Variety • Expressiveness • Originality • Creativity	Writing makes a stereotypical response to the topic; it may contain clichés. Writing lacks energy and personal engagement. The voice of the writer is unclear or generic. Writing lacks audience appeal in its current form. Language is simple. Originality is lacking.		Poem is highly individual and expressive of the writer. The writer express energy for the topic. Vivid language conveys meaning in the writer's own voice. Writing has audience appear — it would do well read aloud. Words are chosen for effect. The writer may experiment with poetic devices such as metaphor or simile. Sensory language is included. The writer takes risks to use language and expression in original ways.
Organization and Structure • Sequence • Clarity • Focus • Cohesion	There is little or no introduction. Poem loses focus. Structure is difficult to follow. Poetic form is undeveloped. Pattern is simplistic and lacks impact. Ending may be abrupt.		Opening lines draw the reader in. Poem flows smoothly and seems cohesive; it is clear and sequential. Writing is easy to follow. Writer uses line breaks and white space to enhance the meaning. Phrases are varied in length. Pattern is chosen for effect. Poem ends with a satisfying conclusion.
Conventions • Spelling • Punctuation • Grammar	Frequent errors in spelling, punctuation or grammar make the writing difficult to understand. Presentation lacks care.		Basic grammar, spelling and punctuation are correct, but there may be some errors in complex structures. Presentation of writing shows care.

The Senses in Color

Why teach this anchor lesson?

- To show students how to use their senses to engage with the topic and use language vividly
- To help students create powerful imagery with specific examples

Special instructions: Gather a selection of paint chips from a paint store.

How to do it

Session 1: From the generic to the specific

1. Explain to students that poets use their senses to help us see and experience things in a new way.
2. Choose a red paint chip from the collection and engage the class in a discussion about the color. For example:

TEACHER: What does red look like?
STUDENT: Red looks like a cherry.
TEACHER: Where do you see this cherry?
STUDENT: Red as a cherry on an ice-cream sundae.
TEACHER: What does red taste like?
STUDENT: Red tastes like hot sauce.
TEACHER: Tell me more about that hot sauce.
STUDENT: The Tabasco sauce on my dad's hot dog smells red, red, red.
TEACHER: What else might red look like?
STUDENT: Red looks like fire.
TEACHER: When is fire the reddest?
STUDENT: Red is the flames from a dragon.

The teacher's interactions with the students' ideas are critical here. The teacher moves the contributions from generic to specific by asking questions such as these: When do you see that? Where would that be? When is that the most intense feeling?

3. Record students' ideas on the board and help students to stretch their thinking.
4. Continue in this way, refining and extending student contributions to create specific and powerful images. Below is a poem created by one class that went through this process.

What is red?

Red is a cherry on an ice cream sundae
Red is Tabasco sauce on a hot dog —
No thanks!
The flames from a dragon are red,
So is a strawberry and
a nose bleed.
My heart beats red at the end of a race
"I hate you!" is the sound of red
Strength, anger and intensity
That's the feeling of red.

Session 2: From paint chips to strong images

1. Put the class poem from the previous day on an overhead or a chart.
2. Ask students: Which ideas are most powerful? Why do you think so?
3. Ask students to choose a paint chip from the collection to write about. They meet in talking pairs to develop preliminary ideas. You can lead the discussion by asking partners to respond to the following prompts:

   - When is your color the strongest, the clearest, the most delicate?
   - If your color was an emotion, what feeling would it be? When would you experience it?
   - If your color was something you could touch, what would it feel like?
   - If your color was a taste, what would it be? When would you taste it best?

4. Individually, students use a thinking page (see Blackline Master 4.1) to begin a list of possibilities that represent their chosen paint chip color. (A thinking page can also be seen as a worksheet or rough working paper.)
5. Students select their most powerful images and draft them into a poem.
6. Once they have done so, they can meet informally to share poems with each other.

> Remember the writing anchors: Use your five senses. Make it your own!

While students are writing, circulate and prompt students with questioning to add detail and description. Stop the class and ask students to share aloud their writing gems. Do this with caution, however, to avoid a class set of identical poems and to avoid disrupting students' thinking too often.

Student Reflection

- What are your favorite images? Read them aloud to a partner.
- What did you learn in this lesson that you can use in Writing Workshop?

Evaluation

To what extent was the student able to
– use the senses to create original images?
– move beyond generic writing to capture vivid, specific images?

Richard's poem creates an impact on the reader and his words are chosen for effect: "old tin can in a dark basement."

In this student sample Claris juxtaposes many ideas and images related to the color blue. She uses both concrete and abstract ideas to make an impact on the reader, taking risks to use language in original ways.

The Color of Kings and Sapphire Rings

Blue is the color of a meteor shower,
A revolution,
A little pit of power.
The deep blue sea
The eyes of some people like me.
A cold-blooded heart,
The inside of a blueberry tart.

A crocus is blue
Some butterflies, too,
A color in many a flag,
Also in a dishcloth rag.
A waterfall that gently flows
Into a river which you hang your toes
The color of kings and
Sapphire rings,
A bluebird flying, a flurry of wings.

The silhouette of a wolf drinking moonlight
The truth that lives in a solemn, loyal plight.
Blue is the color of a mermaid's skin,
The color splashed on a great whale's fin.
The color of holding on and not letting go
The blue sky we wish to better know
The light that shines when all is dark
The colored slide that perfects the park.
A sword fight between good and bad
A hat belonging to a Scottish lad
The color of a blazing hot fire
The feel of your breath when you begin to tire.
A color that will always be
The color that is truly wild and free.

By Claris

Things I Love

Why teach this anchor lesson?

- To show students how to choose specific language and sensory images to give the writing "voice"

How to do it

Session 1: Exploring voice

1. Explain that poets write with voice — a unique style that shows the writer's personality. When a poem has strong voice, you can often tell who the poet is, even without the writer's name on it.
2. Lead the class in a discussion much like the following.

   TEACHER: How many of you like cookies? Almost everyone. Right. So if we write in our poem "I like cookies" then it could be anybody's poem. When you are using your writer's voice you must tell about the cookies you like best. Paul, you like cookies. What kind of cookies are your favorite?

   PAUL: I like chocolate cookies.

   TEACHER: When do you eat them?

   PAUL: I like chocolate cookies after school with a glass of milk.

   TEACHER: There! See! Now we can hear Paul's voice. It's not an "anybody poem" anymore. I prefer chewy oatmeal cookies with raisins. They taste great with a glass of lemonade. Paul and I have very different ideas about cookies. You want to show how you are unique by letting us hear your writer's voice.

3. Further model your favorite things aloud, taking care to speak about the specifics that make your ideas unique.
4. Engage the students in partner talk about their favorite things. Ask: What do you love to feel on your skin? When does it feel best? What do you love to see in the sky? When does it look just perfect? What do you love to taste? Who makes it just the way you like it? And so forth.
5. Students work on the Things I Love Thinking Page, taking time to expand their ideas to give them voice (see Blackline Master 4.2).

Circulate to prompt students' thinking.

TEACHER: I see you like waterfalls. Tell me more.
Student writes: I love misty waterfalls crashing down the mountainside.

TEACHER: I love ice cream too. What's your favorite?
Student writes: I love almond fudge ice cream in a waffle cone.

Session 2: Being specific

1. Students return to their thinking pages and begin to draft poems.
2. Conference with students to help edit their poems and give them shape.
3. Students publish their revised poems and read them to one another in small groups.
4. You may compile them in a class book.

> Remember the writing anchors: Use your five senses. Make it your own!

Student Reflection

- When you want to let readers hear your writer's voice, what do you need to remember to do?
- What will you use from this lesson in Writing Workshop?

Evaluation

To what extent was the student able to
– use specific language to give his or her writing voice?

In this sample from a younger student, we hear Richard talk about things he loves. He expands each idea to add details making the poem individual and expressive of the writer.

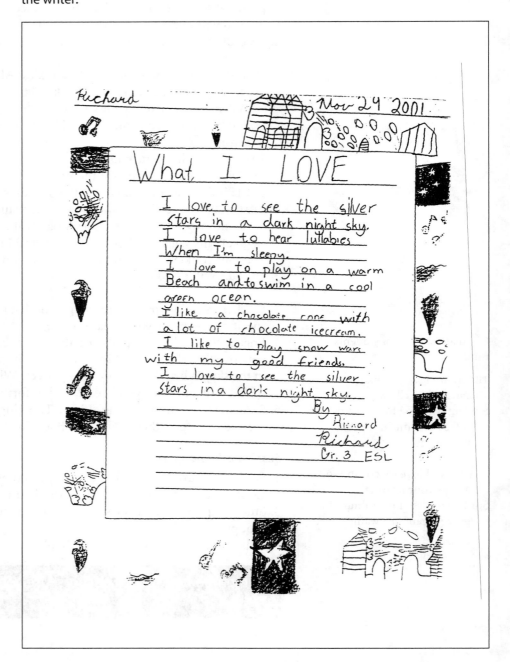

Alex's poem is rich with personal voice. We can smell the roast beef and our mouths begin to water as the Grade 5 student describes the dinner.

Dinner

I can smell the delicious aromas of roast beef
It is coming out of the oven
My mouth waters with anticipation
The yorkshire pudding is almost ready
And now . . .
We sit down to
Yorkshire pudding
Roast beef
Mashed potatoes
And a gallon of gravy!

As I take the first bite
A glorious flavour pours into my mouth
I try to remember
What was in that magnificent meaty marinade?
More please.

Another delicious dozen Yorkshire puddings come into the room
please pass the Yorkshire pudding
one guest says

After that we have dessert

Chocolate cake
Lemon meringue pie
and three varieties of ice cream
More please.

By Alex

The Five Senses and the Weather

Why teach this anchor lesson?

- To show students how to choose specific language, details, and sensory images to give the writing voice
- To show students that revisiting and revising writing creates a more powerful piece

How to do it

Session 1: A sensory walk

1. Identify the five senses and explain to students that they are going on a walk to experience the weather with all their senses. This activity would be good to do on a day when the weather is particularly dramatic — a very windy day or an exceptionally cold day would lead to interesting observations.
2. Take students for a walk outside to observe the weather using all their senses.
3. Return to class so that they can discuss their images in talking partners. Prompt student talk by asking questions: What does it feel like? look like? sound like? smell like? taste like? Talk about developing the writer's voice and creating vividness by moving the writing from generic expression to personal, detailed expression.

GABRIELLE: Snow covers the playground like a blanket.
TEACHER: What blanket are you thinking of?

Together they develop: Snow covers the playground like Grandma's quilt.

JERRY: Snow feels cold on my fingers.
TEACHER: What do your fingers look like when you touch snow?

Together they develop: Snow turns my bare fingers to cramped claws.

4. Students begin to draft ideas on thinking pages. (See BLM 4.3.)
5. Circulate to help students who are stuck and to highlight good examples. Pause to probe student thinking and extend ideas.

Session 2: Choosing images

1. Ask selected students to read aloud their best ideas.
2. Remind students that great ideas come from personal images and specific details rather than lists of adjectives. For example: "Snow turns the tree branches to chandeliers in an ice palace" is better than "White, fluffy snow covers the thin, brown branches."
3. Tell students to go back to their thinking pages and choose their favorite ideas to develop into a poem with specific language.

Remember the writing anchors: Use your five senses. Make it your own!

Student Reflection

- Choose an example that demonstrates how you chose your words carefully to reveal your voice in your poem.
- What did you learn from this lesson that you can use in Writing Workshop?

Evaluation

To what extent was the student able to
- use the senses to develop original ideas?
- use specific language to give the writing voice?
- and willing to revise the writing to create a more powerful piece?

This student work shows the process of planning and drafting a poem. Christopher selects those ideas he likes the best and orders them to create a sensory poem.

Planning Page for On a Rainy Day
Christopher 05/21/2003

Feels like feels like a ladybug touching me
Feels like a rolling ball rolling on my hand
Feels like a tickle from a peice of my hair ✓
Tiny pebble falling on my hand

Smells like roses that I picked up from a rocky floor ✓
my grass in the back yard
my peice of paper that I'm just wri

Looks like small tiny face that smiles at me ✓
eyes that look at me and everybody
bullet rushing down from the sky

Tastes like a sprinkle of water on my tongue
drip of a cool peice of snow
a tiny taste of bitter juice ✓

Sounds like foot steps walking in a rythm ✓
on the floor broken glass smashing
an earaser falling on my school de

What I like to do jump in the puddles makeing the water splash around me
droping petals from a rose in a pu
making ripples ✓

On a Rainy Day

Feels like a tickle from a piec
of my hair,

Smells like roses that I picked
up from a rocky floor,

Looks like a small tiny face
that smiles at me,

Tastes like a tiny taste of
bitter juice,

Sounds like my foot steps
walking in a rythm,

I like to drop petals from
a rose in a puddle making
ripples,

Christopher Gr 3

105

Using Poet's Eyes

Jonathan London writes books that are rich with metaphor and simile. If you can locate one of the following to read aloud, it will create a powerful model for students: *Like Butter on Pancakes* or *The Condor's Egg*.

Special instructions: Obtain a cactus, possibly from a dollar store, and a collection of sea shells.

Why teach this anchor lesson?

- To show students how to create vividness and use expressive language using metaphor and simile

How to do it

1. Lead the class in a discussion on ways in which poets use language and look at the world in new ways. Highlight examples of original thinking in poems familiar to the class. For example, in Jonathan London's *Like Butter on Pancakes*, this image appears: "and the spoons sleep nestled in the kitchen drawer."
2. Tell the students that anyone can see the world through "poet's eyes." You look at something in a new way; you see it as if you never saw it before. You think about what the object reminds you of and you see it in a fresh and different way.
3. Show the cactus and invite the class to look at it in a new way. See sample dialogue below.

   TEACHER: What does this cactus look like to you?
   STUDENT: A piece of holly.
   TEACHER: Yes, it's dark green and prickly just like a piece of holly. Let's put that in our poem. What else does it look like?
   TEACHER: What else does it look like?
   STUDENT: The flower on top looks like a bubble gum but it's prickly too.
   TEACHER: Yes, it's all round and lumpy like lots of bubble gum. We can add that to our poem. Remember, a poem has white space. The lines are not written like a story. I will make these lines shorter so I have white space too. Where shall I stop the lines? . . .

4. Continue to build a group poem and construct the images together. Here is the poem that one class wrote:

   What is a cactus?

   A cactus is
   As prickly as a piece of holly
   and as prickly as Hedgie the hedgehog,
   The pink flower on top
   is like
   a bubble gum pincushion.
   Now you know a cactus.

5. Students now look with poet's eyes and see the shell in a different way. Independently, they make images that "tickle the brain."
6. Go to each student in turn, helping them to look, develop images, get started, and so on.

If this is a first lesson with young students, the concept of white space may be difficult to grasp. You could come back to the students' ideas another day and reshape the lines. Or, as they gain familiarity with poetry, bring the varying lengths of lines to their attention.

Student Reflection

- What did you enjoy in your poetry today?
- Which lines are your favorite? Read them to your partner.
- What will you use from this lesson in Writing Workshop?

Evaluation

To what extent was the student able to
– develop images?

In David's poem, we see him take a fresh look at a seashell. He sees it as a whirlpool, a castle for a fairy, a flute and a cave. He enjoys putting ideas together and experiments with similes.

> A Seashell Is . . .
>
> A seashell is
> A home for a
> sweet hermit crab.
> It spins around like a whirlpool
> It's a castle
> For a fairy.
> My seashell is as blue as the sky
> On a hot summer's day,
> As long as a flute for a princess,
> As hollow as a cave for a grizzly bear.
>
> By David

Images in the Environment

Why teach this anchor lesson?

- To show students how to create vividness and use expressive language with metaphor and simile

How to do it

Session 1: A fresh look

1. Explain to students that poets often look at things in ways that "tickle the brain." They take an idea and compare it with something else, for example, a hose pipe with an elephant's trunk; raindrops on a twig with a necklace, fluffy clouds with pillows. When they think of ways in which two things are the same, new ideas come into their minds.
2. Review Blackline Master 4.4 and determine what you want students to focus on in their immediate environment. Take them outside with copies of the planner and pencils. Their job is to capture images from the environment through the senses and to begin metaphors with sentence frames.
3. Bring students inside and have them discuss their focus images with a partner.

Session 2: Powerful images

1. Students sit in partners and read their images aloud. They discuss which are their favorite, most powerful images and why.
2. Students, working alone or in partners, choose a focus for their writing. For example, they could choose trees or mountains. They then develop their images.
3. Students meet with others to share their poems and receive feedback on the most powerful images.
4. Share an example of your own writing done on the theme and show students the number of revisions needed to make the writing powerful. A poem that Janine wrote appears below.

November Sun
White sun,
Cold as a mother's fear,
Poor as a beggar,
Warmth squandered on
 August beaches,
Slips steadily southward
Leaving us frozen in a
 northern land.

Golden son,
Raised in a mother's love,
Rich as a prince,
Savings pinched from tips
 and wages,

In this lesson Janine wrote with the students. She showed the students her thinking and the messiness of her writing as she struggled to express her ideas with the best words and images possible. She also shared the finished piece with them. While they didn't understand many of the images, they were impressed that adults write about their feelings in poems. Joining students in writing and in risk taking validates their efforts as writers.

slips steadily southward
Searching for manhood in
a sun burnt land.

By Janine Reid

5. While students are working hold conferences to help them polish their work.

Remember the writing anchor: Use poet's eyes.

Student Reflection

• What did you learn about writing poetry in this lesson that you can use in Writing Workshop?

Evaluation

To what extent was the student able to
— use the senses, metaphors and similes to generate and shape ideas?

Allison and Melissa not only create interesting similes, they also choose an ending with pizazz. "November trees put on a show for free" evokes the enjoyment these girls felt as they engaged with the topic. Meng Qi features three similes within five lines.

Janine chose to have students work in partners to write drafts of their poems with felt markers on charts scattered throughout the classroom on the floor. Interaction between the students helped to extend their ideas about what is a metaphor and what should be included in their poems.

November Trees

November trees
Are as flexible
As acrobats
As tall as an elephant
As wiggly as a loose tooth
As long as a necklace.
They are an umbrella full of food for all.
The leaves are
Turning, turning, turning.
November trees
Put on a show for free.

By Allison and Melissa

November Trees

The trees cool me like a fan
The leaves fall down
Like the feathers from a bird.
The leaves change colour
Like a snake changing its skin.

By Meng Qi

More about Metaphors and Similes

Why teach this anchor lesson?

- To show students how to create vividness and use expressive language with original ideas and images, using "poet's eyes"
- To teach the importance of thinking by metaphor and analogy to create an impact for the reader

How to do it

Special instructions: Make available magnifying glasses, jeweller's loupes or windows cut in black paper. These devices help to change the scale of an object in order to help students develop metaphors, similes and analogies.

1. As part of a warm-up, allow students to experiment and play with the loupes or windows to find a focus and learn how to use them.
2. Students choose a focus object and look closely to draw the detail. Objects from nature — blossoms, shells, snails, fruit, vegetables and more — work well. Fine-tip black markers may be supplied for drawing.
3. As students continue to look, ask them to develop a list of ideas, or a thinking page. Prompt their thinking with questions like these: What does this remind you of? What else does it look like? If you were this tiny, what would you use it for? If it had a fragrance, what would it be like? If it had a taste, what would it taste like? Who might live there? Ask some students to share their ideas aloud. Probe the ideas to expand them.

Once, when looking at a blossom, my students wrote "bed" and "dress." I reminded the students of other anchor lessons about expanding their ideas. When I prompted a student to think of who would use that bed, she wrote: "A blossom is a bed for the king and queen of the fairies."

4. Students return to their thinking pages to select their powerful ideas. Remind students to use their "poet's eyes" to see things in a new way and to expand their ideas to create images that "tickle the brain." It's time for them to draft their poems.

> **Remember the writing anchor: Use poet's eyes.**

Student Reflection

It is helpful for some students to provide an opening and closing sentence to frame the poem. See examples for structuring poetry on pages 95 to 96.

- What are your most powerful images? Share them with a classmate.
- How did you come up with your images? Talk about your thinking.
- What did you learn from this anchor lesson today that you can use in Writing Workshop?

Evaluation

To what extent was the student able to
– use the strategy to shape work with evidence of metaphor and simile?

Intermediate students may be able to explain why they think of their object as they do. For example, "When I look inside a blossom I see fireworks exploding because blossoms explode in the spring." We have found primary students do not often seem capable of making that leap into theorizing and are satisfied to develop their poems from their simple images.

This young student is learning to compare images and find new ways to describe what he sees.

> 1.Y
> 23. When I look
>
> When I look
> in to a blossom
> I see clam shells
> and small base
> balls in the air.
> I can see Butterfly wing
> flying in the air
> and small boats sailing
> on a cotton candy sea.
> When I look into
> a blossom
> I think of a fire
> crackers becase blossoms
> explode in the spring.
>
> Wesley   ESL

This is one of our favorite student poems. Katie has observed the ponderous movement of snails and expressed original and creative ideas.

What is a snail?

What is a snail?
A snail is an octpus
Dragging his food along,
A snail is a shy child
On his first day of school.
A snail is a tired parent
After a long day of work.

How does a snail move?
A snail moves like someone
Swimming at the end
Of a marathon,
A snail moves like someone
Riding a bike uphill.
A snail moves like someone
Lifting a very heavy weight.
That is what a snail is.
By Katie

Poetry Cut-ups: Playing with Words

Why teach this anchor lesson?

- To show students how to choose words carefully for effect

How to do it

Special instructions: Prepare flashcards for the words listed on Blackline Master 4.5. Students will also need photocopies of the blackline master.

1. Explain to students that poets choose their words carefully to create a mood or express a feeling.
2. Distribute the flashcards to students, about one per student.
3. Construct a group poem in a pocket chart by asking students to contribute cards that make sense and create interesting images as in the following scenario:

TEACHER: You each have a card with a word on it. Together we are going to use some of the words to create poems that play with words and images. I am going to get us started by choosing the word "wolf." Who has a word that can go with wolf?

STUDENT: I have the word "the."

TEACHER: Great. We'll put the words "The wolf" in the pocket chart. Now what is the wolf doing?

STUDENT: I have the word "watches."

TEACHER: "The wolf watches." What is he watching? What is happening while he watches?

Teacher and students continue to build the poem together. Here is one that a class devised:

> The wolf watches
> Wind and shadows wild
> Move across the snow
> Whispering "join me."

I taught this lesson the first time with ESL students who couldn't tell the difference between playful imagery and gobbledegook. Next time, I photocopied nouns and verbs on different colors of paper and demonstrated how images need to have a noun and a verb to make sense.

4. Distribute photocopies of Blackline Master 4.5 for each student to cut up.
5. Students select a few words and experiment with them, adding, discarding, trading, and creating new ones until they shape a poem.
6. Students copy or paste words onto paper.
7. Bring students together to share their poems.

To extend the lesson, you might challenge students to see how many variations they can make on a theme, for example, dreams.

Remember the writing anchor: Play with words!

Student Reflection

- What did you enjoy in this activity?
- What did you learn in this lesson that you could use in Writing Workshop?

Evaluation

To what extent was the student able to
– manipulate words to experiment with expressive language?
– create original poetry ?

Sophie's poem is a good example of the sort of writing this process can lead to.

Happiness Is Your Key

Join me, shadow wolf
Roar wildly to the stars.
Awaken the wind's dreams.
Spring toward the sun.
Let tomorrow hold you.

Burst across golden plains.
Excitement will guide your joy.
Soar on a rainbow.
Unlock the door, wolf.
Happiness is your key.

By Sophie

Jodie's poem is another good example of the way original ideas can result when students play with words.

If I Had One Wish

If I had one wish
I would be a porpoise and
Swim
In the deep blue tropical waters,
Visit
Wonderful, aquatic life,
Dart like an arrow from
Sea to see.
Explore
Mysterious underwater caves and grottos,
Drift
Lazily among green seaweed,
Weave
Through bright coral,
Dance
With frolicking seahorses,
Scamper
With jumbo shrimp,
Shake
With long, slender eels.
Skim
The sand with skittish lobsters and crabs,
Play

Hide and seek with shy clams and oysters,
Tickle
Cute little starfish
Poke
Spiny, globular sea urchins
Mander
With floral sea anemones,
Float
With transparent, ghostlike jelly fish,
Glide
With wide, flat stingrays,
Roam
With rainbow coloured exotic fish and
Mingle
With smiling dolphins and
Singing whales as they
Gracefully cruise the oceans.
If I Had One Wish.

By Jodie

Repetition Heightens Impact

Why teach this anchor lesson?

- To show students how to expand their writing on the dimensions of Engagement with the Topic, Vividness and Language Use, and Organization and Structure to create an impact on the reader with repetition of a word, a line or a refrain

How to do it

Session 1: A demonstration

1. Explain to students that poets often use repetition in their writing to give it coherence and add impact.

2. Ask students to suggest a topic for your demonstration, as in the scenario below:

   TEACHER: What kind of experiences can you suggest that we might write about? Can you think of some things that we all do?
   STUDENT 1: Playing at recess.
   STUDENT 2: Doing homework.
   STUDENT 3: Going swimming.
   TEACHER: Thank you. Let's choose recess as our topic. Turn to a classmate and tell your partner what you love to do at recess.

3. Continue to prompt student pairs with questions:

   - What are the sounds you hear at recess time?
   - What are some action words that you could use to tell about recess?
   - What do you love to taste at recess?
   - What feelings do you have at recess?

4. Engage the class in constructing a poem using repetition of parts of speech, similes, phrasing and single words to add impact. One class constructed this poem:

   Recess

   Zooming
   Like a speeding bullet
   Skipping, chatting, shouting

   Recess
   Racing
   Like a cheetah
   Chasing, screaming, laughing

   The best part of school
   Recess

5. Ask students to choose a topic and begin drafting their writing. While they are at work, write a poem about recess to share with the class later on.

Session 2: Writing refrains

1. Students revisit their thinking pages to select their best ideas and a phrase for repetition. Now it's time for them to develop their own poems.

> Remember the writing anchor: Play with words!

Student Reflection

- What will you remember from this lesson for your work in Writing Workshop?

Evaluation

To what extent was the student able to
– use a refrain to add coherence to their work?
– refine and polish ideas?

Sam, a student with special needs, dictated this poem to his education assistant. The focus on sounds, as well as the repetition, result in a poem that all the students appreciated.

Playground

squeak squeak
the swings go up and down
drop drop
the rain falls from the sky
ha ha ha
the children laugh
stomp stomp
the children jump
mumbo jumbo
the children talk
clap clap
the children play
       By Sam

If You're Not from the Prairie, by David Bouchard, provided a model for this repetitious refrain.

Have you seen Vancouver?

Have you seen monstrous mountains covered with snow
like a soft white blanket?
Have you seen maple trees as red

as cherries in spring?
Have you seen the long city sidewalks
bustling with people as busy as a beehive,
as loud as a siren?
Have you seen Vancouver?

Have you seen the beaches with its sand
like glittering diamonds and crashing waves?
Have you seen the tall skyscrapers
almost touching the moon?
Have you seen the skytrains whizzing by as fast as lightning?
Have you seen Vancouver?

Have you seen Granville Island's Crystal Ark
with sparkling rocks and crystals?
Have you seen the Aquarium
with the big fish staring at you with their
glassy eyes?
Have you seen the colourful sunset
shining at night like the bright lights on a stage?
Have you seen Vancouver?

                                    By Chris

The Magic Box

On occasion, the work of published poets can provide us with springboards or frameworks for our own writing. Two good examples are "Life Doesn't Frighten Me" by Maya Angelou and "Mother Doesn't Want a Dog" by Judith Viorst. The poem that we are featuring here is Kit Wright's "The Magic Box," published in *Cat Among the Pigeons*. We have used it with great success.

Why teach this anchor lesson?

- To develop students' use of sensory imagery
- To introduce alliteration as a poetic device
- To scaffold the creation of an original poem by using a published work

How to do it

1. Read the chosen poem several times with the class. ("A Magic Box" appears on the next page.) Play with the poem orally through choral reading. Enjoy the sound of the words, the alliteration and the repetition.
2. After reading, discuss with the class what they like about the poem. What images are successful? Which language "tickles the brain"? Does anything puzzle them or seem difficult to understand? If using "A Magic Box," elicit from the class the following points: the poet uses sensory images such as "the swish of a sari" and "a rumbling belly"; one effective use of alliteration is "the tip of a tongue touching a tooth." Ask the class if they notice anything special about the stanzas or verses. (Each one has its own theme, including a reversed world in verse four; the last two verses describe the box and what the writer will do with it.)
3. Using these ideas, the students begin to draft their own first verses. A collection of photographs may prompt ideas, too.
4. After the class has had time to draft one verse, ask for one as a working sample and write the verse on the chalkboard or chart. Invite the class to revise the verse as a group, adding alliteration or crafting an image.
5. Ask the students to revise their own first verses, making at least one change.
6. Students read their poems to a partner. Poems could be illustrated when finished. Each poem could also be placed in shoe box — a magic box — decorated with the images chosen.

> Remember the writing anchors: Use poet's eyes. Use your five senses. Make it your own!

Student Reflection

- As you wrote, what did you find that worked? What was helpful?
- What is one thing you really like in your poem? Explain why.
- What do you think you will remember that will be useful in Writing Workshop?

Evaluation

To what extent was the student able to
- show originality in the poem?
- create an impact on the reader with language and images?
- choose words with care?

THE MAGIC BOX

I will put in the box
the swish of a silk sari on a summer night,
fire from the nostrils of a Chinese dragon,
the tip of a tongue touching a tooth.

I will put in the box
a snowman with a rumbling belly,
a sip of the bluest water from Lake Lucerne,
a leaping spark from an electric fish.

I will put into the box
three violet wishes spoken in Gujarati,
the last joke of an ancient uncle,
and the first smile of a baby.

I will put into the box
a fifth season and a black sun,
a cowboy on a broomstick
and a witch on a white horse.

My box is fashioned from ice and gold and steel,
with stars on the lid and secrets in the corners.
Its hinges are the toe joints of dinosaurs.

I shall surf in my box
on the great high-rolling breakers of the wild Atlantic,
then wash ashore on a yellow beach
the colour of the sun.

Source: "The Magic Box" by Kit Wright in *Cat Among the Pigeons.* © by Penguin Books Ltd. Reprinted by permission of Penguin Book Ltd.

"Sarah's Magic Box" contains the student's original images. Her word choice surprised us when we first read this poem. The poet's own voice can be clearly heard.

Sarah's Magic Box

I will put in the box
A drip of the first sunlight
A splash of color from an evening sunset
A heroic unicorn standing over the land

I will put in the box
The sense of a special silence filled with suspense
A snapshot of the future
A thief who only steals happiness

I will put into the box
The fresh air in the farmer's fields

The smell of new mown hay
Going outside on a rainy day

I will put into the box
A rainbow of ribbon or a forest of faith
How about a prison of freedom
Or a gold goblet of fire to melt your tears

My box has a lid embroidered with jewels
It is of special stone that changes with the weather
It has a lock of sterling
Only to be undone by love

I shall thrive with my box
It shall bring me all the joys of the world
But then in a while I'll die
I'll put my spirit in my box.

Miles puts a different spin on "The Magic Box." His interest in fantasy is evident.

Mile's Magic Box

I will put into the box
the brightness from lake of happiness
the darkness from forest of silence
and the lava from my best nightmare.

I will put into the box
a grunt of an ancient cyclops
the fire from Greek Chimera
and a riddle of great sphinx.

I will put into the box
the treasure from dreadful mountain
the venom of gigantic cobra
and the darkness of the sun.

I will put into the box
the great blizzard over the Sahara
the sand blast over the Antarctica
and the shark from sky.

My box is fashioned from horns of dragons and feathers from a phoenix
with jewels from chimera on the lid and riddles in the corner
its hinges are the jawbone from the crocodile.

I shall swim in my box
on the great giant of lost world
then dig all the way through the earth
with great shovel.

Show, Don't Tell: Think of a Time

Students' vocabulary for emotions is often limited to *mad, sad, bad,* and *glad.* In this anchor lesson students will learn that a powerful poem can show a feeling without using the words for the feeling.

Why teach this anchor lesson?

- To show students how to convey emotion "between the lines" through effective word choice
- To show students how the placement and shape of a poem contribute to its meaning

How do do it

Session 1: Guided imagery

1. Lead students in a guided imagery session. Students close their eyes and try to envision what you are saying. For example:

   "It is minutes before your birthday party. You have invited your best friends to come to your house. You are wearing your favorite outfit. The house is decorated. Your mother has the cake hidden in a large white box tied carefully with string. Presents from your family nestle in gift bags bursting with tissue paper. Games are planned; the food is ready.

   "Imagine this scene in your mind. How are you feeling? Yes, of course you are happy . . . but think deeper. How does happy feel? What does a happy feeling do to your body? your hands? your face? Put yourself in that body and remember the sensations. What are you saying to yourself?

   "You are excited too. How does excited feel? What does an excited feeling do to your body? your hands? your face? Put yourself in that body and remember the sensations. What are you saying to yourself?

   "You might be a little nervous. How does nervous feel? What does a nervous feeling do to your body? your hands? your face? Put yourself in that body and remember the sensations. What are you saying to yourself?

   "Ding dong! There's the first friend at the door!"

2. Engage students in a discussion about their feelings and sensations. In partners, students share their thoughts in response to the following prompts:

   - What did you see in your mind?
   - Tell your partner what you feel like when you are happy.
   - Who would be coming if your party was tomorrow?
   - Tell your partner what you feel like when you are excited.
   - Tell your partner what you feel like when you are nervous.
   - What are you wondering?

   And so forth.

3. Lead the group in thinking aloud about how to convey the feelings about the birthday without using simple descriptors. Write these sentences on the board, taking one line for each: It's my birthday. I am happy. I feel excited. I feel nervous.

   TEACHER: Let's take out the word "happy" and show how happy feels. What happens to you when you are happy?
   STUDENT: I can't stop smiling.

TEACHER: Terrific. What's that like?

STUDENT: Sometimes I smile so much my face hurts.

TEACHER: Great ideas that show your feelings. Now let's take out the word "excited" and see if we can show why we are excited and how that feels.

And so forth. Together, one class wrote the following:

> It's my birthday
> I can't stop smiling,
> So much my cheeks are sore.
> Friends are coming any minute
> I jump and jump
> and jump.
> Will they bring me presents?
> Will they like the hotdogs?
> My tummy flip flops
> There's the door!

4. Explain to students that they need to collect thoughts for writing. Students do not have to write about a birthday, but it would help to think of a time with emotional intensity. Fear? Anger? Peace?
5. Students pause to consider their moment.
6. Have students engage in partner discussions about the time they have in mind. Prompt students again to consider the images, feelings and sensations they experienced.
7. Students begin to collect ideas on a planning page, identifying the event in the centre of a web and the images, feelings and sensations associated with it on connecting rays.

Session 2: Reshaping class poem

1. Review the last session and the big idea "Show, Don't Tell."
2. Revisit the poem to demonstrate how its shape and the placement of the words also convey meaning. Things to consider include placement of line breaks, isolation of words for emphasis, and actions suggested by the words themselves: for example, *down* can be written

> D
> O
> W
> N

See how the class showed active verbs in their revision of the birthday poem.

> Excitement
>
> It's my
>   BIRTHDAY!
> I can't stop smiling,
> So much my cheeks
> are sore.

Friends are coming
any minute!
I
        jump
               and
                        jump
and
      jump.
Will they bring me presents?
Will they like the hotdogs?
My tummy
      flip

There's the door!

3. Set students to work on their images and drafts.
4. Students meet for informal sharing.

> **Remember the writing anchors: Tell the inside and outside stories. Show, don't tell. Give it shape.**

Student Reflection

- What part of this lesson was fun for you?
- What did you learn in this lesson that you can use in Writing Workshop?

Evaluation

To what extent was the student able to
– convey emotions indirectly through careful word choice?
– use white space to convey their meaning?

In these student samples, we see some interesting ways of using the position of words on the page, punctuation and onomatopoeia. The "Gecko" thinking page and poem are written by a Grade 2 student; the second poem, by a Grade 5 student.

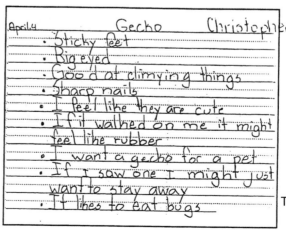

Thinking Page

123

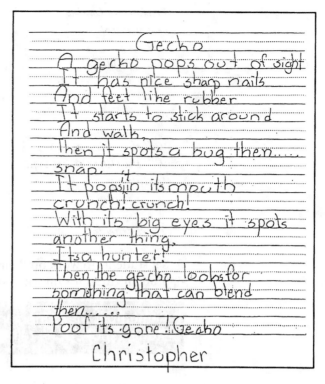

Gecko

A gecko pops out of sight
It has nice sharp nails
And feet like rubber
It starts to stick around
And walk,
Then it spots a bug then....
snap,
It pops in its mouth
crunch! crunch!
With its big eyes it spots
another thing,
It's a hunter!
Then the gecko looks for
something that can blend
then......
Poof it's gone! Gecko

Christopher

The Swinging Rope

The blue rope
h
a
n
g
s
on my cherry tree in the backyard

It feels rough all over except on the
end
where there is smooth yellow tape
with a big blue knot
underneath it.

The blue rope is never still,
Always swaying,
            calling me
                        calling me
"Come   for   a
                  r
                       i
                            d
                                 e!
                              By Alison

Senses in Color Thinking Page

Name: _____ Date: _____

(*your color*)

Sights _____

_____

Sounds _____

_____

Tastes _____

_____

Touches _____

_____

Smells_____

_____

Emotions _____

_____

Seasonal and weather ideas _____

_____

Family members of the color (e.g., Red is a big sister to pink) _____

_____

_____

Things I Love

Name:_____ Date:_____

1. My favorite things to see:

   _____

   _____

2. My favorite things to hear:

   _____

   _____

3. My favorite things to smell:

   _____

   _____

4. My favorite things to feel:

   _____

   _____

5. My favorite things to make:

   _____

   _____

6. My favorite time of year/day:

   _____

   _____

7. My favorite place to be:

   _____

   _____

The Five Senses and the Weather Thinking Page

Name:_____ Date:_____

Feels like

Smells like

Looks like

Tastes like

Sounds like

What I like to do

Images in Our Environment Planner

looks like

is the color of

moves like

feels like

What is it doing?

Why?

Other

looks like

is the color of

moves like

feels like

What is it doing?

Why?

Other

look like

are the color of

move like

feel like

What are they doing?

Why?

Other

look like

are the color of

move like

feel like

What are they doing?

Why?

Other

Poetry Cut-ups

Name:_____   Date:_____

to burst open	wolf	toward
bubbles	shadow	across
spring	door	soar
golden	happiness	wind
joy	awake	wolf
excitement	dreams	tomorrow
burst	keep	whisper
sun	hold	roar
join me	crowd	stars
rainbow	explodes	wild

5

Writing Narrative

Anchor Lesson	Skill Focus
A Traditional Tale Uncovered • Building background knowledge • Sequencing events • Using drama • Using a story grammar • Writing traditional tales	Understanding story elements; recognizing story grammar; building a beginning, middle and end
Circular Stories: Beginnings and Endings • Picture book patterns • Revising stories	Connecting beginnings and endings
Rebus Story: The Night I Followed the Dog	Drawing the reader in and ending with pizazz
Writing in Role	Understanding the relationship between problem and solution
Listen, Draw, Write • Pictures from words • Storyboarding and beyond	Understanding the relationship between problem and solution
The First Little Pig	Developing the inside and outside stories
Show, Don't Tell: Describing How Characters Feel • Identifying feelings • Finding passages • Revising	Developing detail
The Button Jar	Creating characters; developing detail; writing dialogue
My Imagination Is My Guide: Using Guided Imagery	Building on sensory experience
Through Different Eyes • Observing what's around us • Writing as ants	Taking a new perspective

Story is important in the lives of young children. Arthur Applebee notes that children's sense of the story form seems to develop very early in life and is evident in their language by the age of two. By the age of four or five, they are able to manage the narration of quite long and involved stories which emerge in their imaginative play. A story links events together in a narrative sequence and gives them a coherence and significance. A story has a form that is universal. As Kieran Egan puts it in *Primary Understanding*, "It has a beginning, which sets up expectation, a middle that complicates it, and an ending that satisfies or resolves it."

Children are natural storytellers and through their storytelling, perhaps create an accessible, meaningful and understandable environment in which to make sense of the real world. Through the imagination, they wrestle with abstractions such as good and evil, bravery and cowardice, hope and despair, right and wrong. Egan says that they "fix an affective response to events and determine the meaning of their contents" (p. 98). In *The Uses of Enchantment*, Bruno Bettleheim demonstrates the power of traditional stories and folk tales to provide vital psychological structures enabling children to make sense of experience. He points out that "the manner in which the child can bring some order into his world is by dividing everything into opposites." The binary opposites in young children's thinking are manifest in their language and play. Things are big or small; they love or hate, they feel safe or afraid, and so on. The stories they tell reflect the stories they hear. The stories they hear read or told in early childhood help them understand their own lives. The problems faced by characters in stories metaphorically represent the dilemmas that children must resolve. Stories are the "pebbles in the moonlight" shining a path for children as they grow.

James Moffett explained it this way: "Whereas adults differentiate their thought with specialized kinds of discourse such as narration, generalization, and theory, children must, for a long time, make narrative do for all. They utter themselves almost entirely through stories — real or invented — and they apprehend what others say through story."

Understanding Story Grammar

Although storytelling is a natural way for children to organize their world, at the age of six or seven when they come to write stories, they need the support of the teacher in learning the basic structures of *story grammar*. Most simple stories are more complex than they at first seem, but there are some common features. All stories set characters in a time and a place. A problem or goal is the focus of the characters' endeavors. A chain of events leads to the resolution of the problem or the reaching of the goal.

The teacher of writing can help young storytellers through some simple activities that teach the principles of this story grammar: beginning, middle and end; the dynamics of plot; problem and solution; and, as children become more capable, the use of dialogue as a means of advancing plot and establishing character. Instruction about the language of story writing can also help young writers craft their stories. The anchor lessons provided in this resource take the basic principles of story grammar and explore them through a variety of activities.

In the first few lessons, we focus on story sequence, helping students find a satisfactory beginning that sets up the narrative; a middle that develops the plot, and an ending that brings events to a satisfying conclusion. We begin with several activities leading up to the writing of a traditional tale.

The next few anchor lessons address the issue that every good story has a problem or dilemma that needs to be resolved. If students are to write their own stories, they will need to understand the dramatic tension between the problem and the solution.

Students also need to think about the outward appearance and inner characteristics of story characters. Anchor lessons explore the language of behavior, motivation, emotions, choices and decisions as well as descriptive language to convey physical characteristics.

Finally, story writing is enhanced when writers use interesting language, a wide vocabulary, varied sentence structures and poetic features such as simile and metaphor. In the last part of the chapter, the focus is language choice for vivid writing, something that is important for setting and mood.

Every time students write a story, they explore the relationship between all these elements: events, characters, problems, solutions and the sequence of the story as the plot unfolds. Each of these lessons focuses on one aspect, but the whole coherence of the story depends upon all elements coming together. Story writing is a difficult genre and the natural ease with which children tackle story writing, compared with the reluctance of most adults, is always exciting in the classroom. Their freshness and delight in storytelling is to be celebrated.

The role of the teacher in teaching this genre has two essential elements. First, we model good stories through reading them and discussing what makes them work. Second, we help students to realize that in story writing, as in many other forms of writing, less is more. A short, well-crafted tale is more enjoyable to read than a long, rambling story that is hard to follow. This understanding may cramp the style of budding Grade 5 novelists, but the classroom is the place for honing the skills and practising the techniques of the trade. The anchor lessons provide a place to begin. No one would need to teach all these lessons; they overlap and offer choice. Make your choice carefully, to ensure that you teach all the elements, and remember to refer back to writing anchors from other lessons from other genres you have taught.

The Writing Profile for Narrative Writing provides criteria for success in story writing and allows students to set their own goals, as well as providing teachers with a scale for evaluation purposes.

Writing Profile for Narrative Writing

Dimensions of Writing	Undeveloped 1	2-3-4	Fully Developed 5
	At a Glance: The story is brief, hard to understand and unoriginal.		At a Glance: The story is focused, expressive, and easy to read. It shows originality.
Engagement with the Topic • Meaning • Ideas • Details	Text may be unclear or illogical. There is little development of ideas; text is predictable and lacking in originality. Writing does not engage the reader.		The meaning is clear; the story has a structure that the reader can follow. A problem is introduced and solved. Characters are developed and consistent. Detail is used effectively to create the setting and the mood.
Vividness and Language Use • Energy • Passion • Voice • Word Choice • Variety • Expressiveness • Originality • Creativity	Writing lacks energy and personal engagement. Voice of the writer is unclear. Story does not engage the reader. Language is simple. Originality is lacking.		Original ideas may be developed in unusual ways. Rich and vivid language engages readers and keeps them interested. Words are chosen for effect; the writer may experiment with poetic devices such as metaphor and simile. Sensory language is included. Writing could be read aloud easily.
Organization and Structure • Sequence • Clarity • Focus • Cohesion	There is no clear beginning, middle and end. Writing loses focus and is difficult to follow. There are simple repetitive sentence patterns or poorly constructed sentences. Ending may be abrupt.		Writing begins effectively, flows smoothly and is clear and easy to follow. It is cohesive, with transition words used effectively. Sentence length and patterns are varied. Writing ends with a satisfying conclusion.
Conventions • Spelling • Punctuation • Grammar	Frequent errors in sentence structure, spelling, punctuation and grammar make the writing difficult to understand. Presentation is lacking care.		Basic spelling, punctuation and grammar are correct. Presentation of writing shows care.

A Traditional Tale Uncovered

Why teach this anchor lesson?

- To engage students' imagination in the world of folk and fairy tales
- To develop an understanding of story grammar
- To help students build their own stories orally from a series of pictures
- To allow students to create their own original stories based on elements of a traditional tale

How to do it

Session 1: Building background knowledge

1. Over several days, read or tell some traditional stories or fairy tales to the students. After each story read-aloud, discuss with the students the main ideas in each story beginning, middle and end. Summarize and capture these ideas with key words on a piece of chart paper or on the blackboard.

2. Emphasize that all stories have a beginning, which usually introduces the setting, the characters and the problem; a middle, in which the characters take action and the problem is developed (perhaps in several separate episodes); and an ending in which the problem is solved. Traditional tales have a good character (hero) and a bad character (villain). Discuss with the class how we know that the characters are good and bad. Who is the hero and who is the villain in each tale? At this time, you can reinforce the students' understanding of the "Show, Don't Tell" technique. We know the characters by their words, actions, emotions and appearance.

3. Begin a class chart and list the characters, setting, problem and solution for each tale you read. Borrow a collection of folk and fairy tales from the library and as the students read these independently during silent reading, ask them to add details to the chart. A sample appears below.

Title	Characters	Setting	Problem	Solution
The Gingerbread Boy	Old Man, Old Woman, Gingerbread Boy, fox, horse, cow, children	a village long ago	The Gingerbread Boy ran away from the old man and old woman.	They all chased him, but he was eaten by the fox.
The Three Bears	Goldilocks, Papa Bear, Mama Bear, Baby Bear	the three bears' house	Goldilocks helped herself to the bears' things.	The bears came home and Goldilocks ran away.
Red Riding Hood	Red Riding Hood, mother, wolf, grandmother, woodsman	the forest long ago	The wolf wanted to eat grandmother and Red Riding Hood.	The woodsman cut the wolf open with his axe.

Creating an original a story takes much more than one lesson. This sequence of five activities involves reading aloud, oral language work, partner work to rehearse story ideas before writing begins, and the use of a story grammar format. The activities will help students focus on the essential story elements and craft the beginnings, middles and ends of their stories.

Session 2: Sequencing events

1. Choose a picture book story that the students have not heard or read. Choose six or seven illustrations from the story and provide copies for groups of four students to use. Each group gets a set of the illustrations.
2. The students' task is to work together to sequence the pictures, choosing a beginning, middle and end, and to build a story using the clues they see in the illustrations. Allow the groups 15–20 minutes to create the stories.
3. One group at a time takes a turn and presents the stories they have created. They tell the story as a group. Perhaps one student acts as storyteller, or maybe each member of the group tells a portion of the story. Since each group may sequence the pictures in a different order, each story is quite different.
4. When the stories are finished, read aloud the original story. Discuss the ways in which the groups' stories differed from the original. What can students learn to help them in writing their own stories?

Special instructions: For this activity, you will need at least two paperback copies of the same picture book. Keep one copy intact for read-aloud purposes, but cut the other(s) up so that you can mount pictures on cards and laminate them for student use.

Session 3: Using drama to understand the "inside and outside" stories

1. Take a moment from the story you read together. In pairs the students take turns being a character from the story and a newspaper reporter. The reporter interviews the character and probes for details. This improvisation helps students think about how characters speak in their roles. For example:

   REPORTER: Tell me Miss Riding Hood, how did you feel when you saw the wolf coming for you with open jaws?
   RED RIDING HOOD: Well, I was really afraid. I could see his great big pink slobbering tongue and his terrible sharp teeth, and I could smell his horrible breath. I was terrified he was going to swallow me up!

2. Give students the opportunity to share their improvisations with the class.
3. After the drama, ask students to write their conversation as a short dialogue between the two characters. There are two ways to do this: they can write it as a play script or as prose. If you want students to present their dialogues as prose, a mini-lesson on the rules for punctuating dialogue may be needed.

   • Each speaker's words begin on a new line.
   • Punctuation marks are included within the double quotation marks.
   • Emphasize again: Less is more! Student dialogue writing can be lengthy at first. Learning to cut to the essentials is important. Teach "editing out" what is unnecessary.

4. Pairs of students may practise reading the dialogue and presenting a skit in role.

Session 4: Using a story grammar to scaffold a retelling

1. Provide students with a graphic organizer which allows the writer to plan the story before beginning to write. A story grammar organizer is a very useful tool for students to use, as it reminds them of the story elements and prevents them from devoting all their attention to the beginning of the story at the expense of developing the middle and the end. Blackline Masters 5.1 and 5.2 are two versions of graphic organizers. Model with the class how to use one of them with a story you have read together. Episodes can be tricky,

especially when things happen according to the Rule of Three (first, then, finally). Talk about how to synthesize and summarize. This is an exercise in finding the main ideas and eliminating the details.

2. Ask students to analyse a story from a book into its constituent parts on their own.

Session 5: Writing traditional tales

1. Once background knowledge about folk and fairy tales has been established, and the idea of the story grammar is clear, it is time for the students to write their own tales. With older students, there may be more work to do defining the difference between a fairy tale, a folk tale, a myth, a legend and a nursery story. Depending upon the grade level, decide on the type of story you want the students to write. For students who are learning English, or who need a modified program, a retelling of one of the stories that has been shared in class may be appropriate.

2. Using a story grammar organizer such as Blackline Master 5.1 or 5.2, students plan out the events, characters and problem. Have the students share ideas with a friend before writing. A storyboard format, with six boxes, may help them structure their composition. Students may fold a piece of paper into six boxes and number them 1 to 6. They may find it helpful to start by filling in the first and last boxes, identifying the beginning and ending. They then fill in the remaining four boxes with the events of the story.

3. During the story writing, there may be opportunities for mini-lessons that will help students refine their language. Draw upon the anchor lessons the class has already experienced. For example:

   - Using a variety of connecting words (*first, later, afterwards, subsequently, in conclusion*) rather than *and then* (Scaffolding Recount with Smooth Transitions, page 34)
   - Bringing characters to life by describing what they say and do (Show, Don't Tell: Describing How Characters Feel, page 149)
   - Zooming in on a moment in the story; showing the "inside and outside" of the experience, and using descriptive language to bring a moment to life (Zooming In on a Personal Moment, page 31)
   - Using dialogue to add impact (Zooming In on a Personal Moment, page 31)

4. At the end of this story writing unit, it is exciting to publish the stories. Students can make individual books or combine stories in a class book. Once the books are finished, share the stories with a buddy class or hold a parent evening where families can come to celebrate the writing.

Remember the writing anchors: Zoom in! Speak! Show, don't tell. Beginning, Middle and End

Student Reflection

- How did you decide what events fit in the beginning, middle and end?
- How did the story grammar or storyboard help you?
- Does your story have a logical sequence?

- Are your characters described in detail?
- How have you used rich and vivid language to keep your readers interested?

Evaluation

To what extent was the student able to
– write an engaging story which is complete and easy to follow?
– present the events in a logical sequence?
– show an understanding of the elements of a story, including beginning, middle and end?

Here is Grade 4 retelling in storyboard format. Students draw in Box 1 first, then Box 6. Having established beginning and ending, they then fill in the events. This storyboard shows a retelling of *The Reluctant Deckhand*, a novel by Jan Padgett.

This piece of writing is an excerpt from a student's story called "The Land of Dreams."

"Is your story finished?" asked Katie.

"Yup!" replied Grandmother Nicole.

"So fast?" asked Katie.

"So fast? I spent almost a hour telling you the story, well actually, the story only spent half a hour, the other have a hour you spent shouting at me and asking me tons of questions!" joked Grandmother Nicole.

"It was a great story, Grandma, but I am sure that I didn't spend half an hour asking questions! I think it was only 28 minutes! But anyways forgive me for shouting at you," replied Katie.

"It's alright, because when me and my mom saw those people cutting down the trees, I started shouting at her and asking questions too!" said Grandmother Nicole.

"Hey Grandma, how come you remembered every single detail of the story since you had a horrible memory?" asked Katie curiously.

Grandmother Nicole thought for a while, and said, "What did I tell you? I didn't tell you any story! Are you okay, Katie?" asked Grandmother Nicole.

"You know the story about, oh nevermind! Hey why don't we phone those "special" people and tell them to come?" suggested Katie.

"Huh?!" asked Grandma surprisingly. "What in the world are you talking about? Are you sure you're alright?" asked Grandma Nicole.

"Just come with me." said Katie.

After they went inside the house, Katie immediately looked in a huge, thick book trying to find the telephone to contact the "special" person.

Suddenly Grandma Nicole said "136."

"Pardon?" asked Katie.

"Page 136." shouted Grandma.

When Katie turned to 136, she couldn't believe her eyes. It was the page that Katie's been trying to look for. she looks down at the phone number and started dialing. After she hung up, a few minutes later, the "special" people came and started planting. Katie and Grandmother Nicole were so happy.

Two years later, when Katie and Grandmother Nicole went to the forest, they saw beautiful trees with lots of animals living in there. The forest was once again, "The Land of Dreams"

The End!!

Circular Stories: Beginnings and Endings

The original idea for this lesson comes from teacher Carollyne Sinclaire.

Why teach this anchor lesson?

- To draw students' attention to the organization of some stories
- To assist students to write beginnings and endings that connect
- To write powerful leads that draw the reader in, as well as satisfying conclusions
- To practise writing stories with a logical sequence

How to do it

Session 1: Picture book patterns

1. Choose a number of picture books that have beginnings and endings that connect. Often the connection is made by language used in the beginning and echoed in the ending. For example, Nancy Hundal's *I Heard My Mother Call My Name* begins, "I heard my mother call my name and I know I should go in, but it is summer and dusk and beautiful." The ending of the book is simply, "Time to go in." The ending brings the story full circle to a satisfying closure.

2. Read the students a short circular story of your choice and draw their attention to the beginning and ending. We have listed some stories in "Read-Alouds to Motivate Young Authors." Elicit from students how the story is circular, and how the ending and beginning have similarities.

3. Discuss with students how some stories, but not all, connect the beginning of the story to the ending. These connections usually repeat certain words. In some cases, the words are repeated to bring the end of the story back to its beginning, thus bringing the story to a conclusion or a resolution to a problem.

4. Ask students to examine picture books in pairs, looking closely at the beginnings and endings. Prompt them to record these, and tell them to be prepared to talk about how they connect. Are there recurring themes and repeated words or phrases, as well as a satisfying sense of closure to the book? An alternate way to do this activity is to copy the beginnings and endings on two colors of paper. Have the students sort and match the pairs.

Session 2: Revising stories

1. Have students select a suitable piece of their own writing to revise for a circular beginning and ending.

2. Ask the students to examine the opening lines to see if revision is necessary. Does the line draw the reader in? Then have the students look at their endings. What parts could echo the beginning? Which words will they select from the beginning to repeat in the ending? What parts need revision to make them stronger? Ask the students to select powerful words from the beginning to repeat in the ending and revise accordingly.

3. Tell the students to share their writing. Make the repetition of important words from the beginning in the ending the focus for conferences.

4. Prompt students to edit for conventions and make a good copy to display on a bulletin board.

Student Reflection

- What will you remember about this activity?
- How did you try to make your writing connect?

Evaluation

To what extent was the student able to
- write an opening line with sufficient strength to have an impact on the reader?
- connect the beginning naturally with the ending?
- make the ending resonate with the beginning?

Rebus Story: The Night I Followed the Dog

The original idea for this lesson comes from teacher Carollyne Sinclaire.

A rebus is a puzzle in which a word or phrase is represented by pictures, letters or signs representing the original sounds. Below is a sample.

2 YS U R

2 YS U B

 C U R

2 YS 4 me

Why teach this anchor lesson?

- To give students an opportunity to write using different forms (rebus)
- To practise writing stories with a logical sequence
- To focus on beginnings that draw the reader in and on endings that have pizazz

How to do it

1. It is a good idea to ask the school librarian to find examples of rebuses. Alternatively, using a chart, work with the class to create some signs or symbols to illustrate words. Examples: sleep—zzzzzzzz—letters descending as if on a staircase; magical—a picture of a rabbit coming out of a hat. Use the rhyme in the margin.
2. If you have a copy of *The Night I Followed the Dog* by Nina Laden, you can use this to illustrate the idea of a rebus. The author has used a form of this technique in her story. Have you ever wondered what a pet does after its owner goes to sleep? Nina Laden did and wrote a story about it. She invented a secret life for her dog as the owner of a night-club especially for dogs.
3. Tell students that they will be writing their own stories incorporating the theme "The Night I Followed . . ." and using rebus (e.g., The Night I Followed My Teacher, My Bird, My Dad, An Alien). What adventures would their characters have? What secret life would they discover if they followed their character? Brainstorm some ideas before the writing begins.
4. Ask the students, "What would be a good way to open this story? There's an air of mystery about the story. Where is the character going? What will happen as you follow them? Can you establish that mystery in your opening paragraph?" Nina Laden ends her story with the question "It's 10 p.m. . . . Do you know where your dog is?" Discuss the effect of ending a story with a question. Is it an interesting way to end a story, leaving the reader thinking? Suggest that students include a question at the end of their stories.

Remember the writing anchor: Have a hook.

Student Reflection

- Did having a story starter help you write? How?
- Did using rebus affect the words you chose? How?
- Could you use rebus in other writings? When would it be appropriate and when not?
- What seemed to be the effect of using a question at the end of the story?

Evaluation

To what extent was the student able to
– write in a clear and easy-to-follow manner using the rebus technique?
– write events in a logical sequence?
– use an effective question to end the story?
– create a powerful opening lead?

Lisa presents the secret life of her cat in a logical sequence using a limited number of rebus images.

The Night I Followed My Cat

I had a stupid and lazy [cat] . Her name was Polly. [I] don't know why have we brought her. Polly couldn't do a thing. Well, actually she could. She could sleep, eat and make a big mess, but [I] don't know why she always sleep on my [pillow] . And that's kind of [scary] , because when [I] woke up, [I]'ll see her, Right in your [face] . Then, the next day when I woke up, Polly wasn't on my bed! [I] was kind of worried because she wouldn't get down the [stairs] at least you hit her. So [I] looked around for her. Suddenly, [I] heard a noise in the dining room. So opened the [door] slowly and carefully. [I] couldn't believe my [eyes] . Polly had chopsticks in one of her hand, with a [bowl] of rice on the other hand. So closed the [door] and ran away. Just that night, [I] saw Polly secretly ran out of the [door] , [I] decided to follow her. Then [I] notice she was wearing a [shirt] a

142

beautiful 👚. Suddenly, Polly stopped in front of a big 🏠 and she went in. "What is Polly doing here?" 🐱 thought. So 🐱 followed her. 🐱 followed her into a big office, where lots of cats were waiting for Polly! 🐱 can't believe it, she's having a meeting? 🐱 thought. So 🐱 went in. Polly looked at me and said, "What are you doing here?" "Are you talking to me?" 🐱 gulped. "Of course you, who else?" said Polly. Then all of a sudden, all the cats begin to talk. So 🐱 screamed. Then 🐱 woke up. It was only a nightmare, 🐱 thought. Then 🐱 realize that Polly was gone. So I went downstairs to look for her, and 🐱 saw her running out of the 🏠 ! OH NO! NOT AGAIN! 🐱 thought.

By: Lisa

The next two lesson plans help students to understand that the main dynamics of a story reside in the tension between the problem faced by the characters and the way in which this is resolved.

Writing in Role

Why teach this anchor lesson?

- To help students understand the elements of a story by retelling it in role as one of the characters
- To build success as the students do not have to "make up" the story problem
- To understand the relationship between problem and solution

How to do it

1. Read a story to the class that has a clear story structure, a definite problem and clear conclusion.
2. Discuss the characters, setting, problem and solution. Talk about the characters and their feelings at various times in the story.
3. Have the students role-play the story. Three ways of doing it are outlined below.

   Version 1: Have some of the students play the characters in the story. Invite them to come up in role and sit at the front. The rest of the class becomes the audience. Tell the class that they are at a talk show and the guests today are the characters from the story. Introduce the students in-role and begin to ask questions. Focus on the problem in the story. Ask the characters about the problem and how it was resolved.

   The audience thinks of more questions to get the characters talking. Students ask them about their actions, their motivations, and their feelings. They should try to ask open-ended questions such as "Why did you do that? Why did you say that? What were you thinking when . . . ?"

   Version 2: The students each take on a role in the story. Create groups of students with three or four people playing each character. As a class, working one group of characters at a time, the teacher leads the students through a retelling which acts out the story.

   Version 3: With the students in partners, one becomes an interviewer from a newspaper; the other assumes a role from the story. The interviewer asks questions that get the character to tell his or her story. "Tell me, what happened when . . . ? What was the problem you were facing? Tell me about how you dealt with this situation?" After a while, change roles and let the interviewers become the characters.

4. After the role-playing activity, the students begin to write as if they were one of the characters. Writing from the first person, they retell the story from that perspective. Students may want to use a story grammar organizer (see Blackline Master 5.1 or 5.2) to record ideas before they write.

Remember the writing anchor: Problem and Solution

Student Reflection

- How did telling the story from the point of view of the characters help you understand the problem in the story?
- What did you learn from this activity?

Evaluation

To what extent was the student able to
– write with original voice?
– sequence the story correctly?
– show how the problem was solved?

Listen, Draw, Write

There are several versions of this activity originating from the book *Creating Classrooms for Authors* by Jerome Harste, Kathy Short and Carolyn Burke. In their version the teacher reads aloud, stopping at several places in the text for the students to draw what they see in their mind's eye. In this adaptation, the focus is on the understanding of the problem and the solution in a story.

Why teach this anchor lesson?

- To help create prior knowledge by drawing based on images from the story
- To develop prior knowledge by working with vocabulary
- To focus on story problems and their solutions

How to do it

Session 1: Pictures from words

1. Choose a story and select 10–15 words or phrases. Introduce the words one at a time. After three or four words, ask the students what pictures are forming in their minds.
2. Introduce two or three more words. Now what pictures do they have? Have they changed?
3. Continue introducing words. When three-quarters of them have been presented, ask the students to draw pictures representing what they see in their imaginations. These should be sketches, taking no more than three or four minutes to produce.
4. Invite students to share the sketches between partners, then give the group the rest of the words.

Session 2: Storyboarding and beyond

1. Working with the words from the last session, have the students group them under headings: Setting, Characters, Problem, Events, Solution. Talk about where they have placed the words and why. Encourage different opinions and decisions.
2. Next, ask students to begin to think about the story that these words might represent. In pairs, they tell each other the story that they have in their heads, being careful to include a story problem. Using a storyboard (a paper folded into six boxes), they plan the sequence of events and then begin to write. Students try to use as many of the words and phrases that were introduced as they can.
3. After sharing their finished stories, they may listen to the original story from which the words were chosen. Let them compare the author's version with their versions. What is the same? What is different?

Remember the writing anchor: Problem and Solution

Student Reflection

- How did sketching help you write your story?
- Were the words and phrases helpful?

Evaluation

To what extent was the student able to
– write a clear and organized story?
– develop the story from a problem to a logical conclusion?

This sample was written by a Grade 2 student in a lesson using *Big Al* by Andrew Clements.

These next three lessons help children learn to describe characters. Establishing a character, describing the character physically and psychologically, and having the character behave and speak consistently within a story are often beyond the reach of younger children. However, some activities that focus on how to talk about characters will help these skills to develop.

The First Little Pig

Using details that enliven the story draws the reader in to experience the moment with the writer. It's like using a magnifying glass to look carefully at a moment in time. The writer zooms in on it, like a camera operator using a close-up shot in a film.

"Imagine you are the first little pig. You have just finished building your house. The last piece of straw has been tucked into place, and you are settling down to have a nice cup of tea. You look around your lovely new home. You see how cozy it is. You are feeling very pleased with yourself. You think how happy you will be in this house."

Why teach this anchor lesson?

- To develop character by zooming in on a moment in time
- To tell the inside and outside stories (feelings and actions)
- To use dialogue to add impact

How to do it

1. Choose a narrative folk tale to illustrate the concept of the inside and outside stories. We will use the Three Little Pigs as it is well known, but doesn't convey much information about the characters.
2. Tell the class that they will be zooming in on the moment when the first little pig is comfortable and pleased with his new home. You may use guided imagery here to take the students into the story in the role of the pig.
3. On a piece of paper folded in half, students draw the pig inside his house, including speech and thought bubbles to reflect what he is saying and thinking. While they are doing this, circulate, pausing to highlight original thinking or to help students who are stuck.
4. In partners, students share their ideas and make suggestions.
5. Next, discuss the events as the wolf arrives at the door. How does the little pig feel as the wolf shouts, "Little Pig, Little Pig, let me come in!"?
6. Students use the second box to draw the little pig trembling inside his house and create speech and thought bubbles to describe what he is thinking and saying as the wolf draws his breath to blow.
7. Once again, circulate and comment on student ideas or offer help to those students who need it. Invite students to share their work and suggestions.
8. Students now write in role as the first little pig. The story could be written by the whole class, using a chart, blackboard or the overhead projector, with everyone contributing ideas, or each student could write a version.

> Remember the writing anchors: Zoom in! Tell the inside and outside stories. Speak!

Student Reflection

- What did you enjoy about the writing today?
- What can you use from this lesson to make your characters more interesting?
- How could you use cartooning in the future to plan your work?

Evaluation

To what extent was the student able to
– bring the situation to life with detail?
– describe the feelings as well as the actions?
– use dialogue to develop the story?

Show, Don't Tell: Describing How Characters Feel

The original idea for this lesson comes from teacher Carollyne Sinclair.

Why teach this anchor lesson?

- To develop an awareness of how authors use voice to develop characterization
- To develop voice in one's own writing

How to do it

Session 1: Identifying feelings

1. Make an overhead transparency of the passages "Showing, Not Telling" (BLM 5.3). Place the transparency on the overhead and ask students to identify the feelings they associate with each. Alternatively, photocopy the passages, and ask students to list the feelings they find.

   - Henry's heart hurt and he cried for an hour.
   - John and Bob jumped up and down. All the hard work the team had done had at last paid off. They were going to the championships.
   - "Oh, not another broken dish!" thought Mary, as she felt a lump grow in her throat. "What will Mom say!"
   - Lindsay reached the classroom door as books tumbled from her arms. She fumbled for the doorknob, knowing she was late for the field trip. Her heart sank as she looked at the empty classroom.

2. Discuss with students how young writers often use attributes that simply *tell* in their writing. Once they revise that work further into descriptive passages that express emotion, the writing becomes more interesting to read. When authors use this kind of language, they are developing character and often plot by using voice or the personality of writing. Tell the students that they are going to go on a search for interesting passages that show rather than tell.

Session 2: Finding passages

1. Select a book that has good Show, Don't Tell passages to use for demonstration. Use sticky notes to identify passages that you will use. Model the activity by reading aloud a passage or making an overhead transparency of the copy and having students identify the feelings shown by the characters. Ask, "What words in the passage helped you to identify the feelings of the character?" Add words to a list on chart paper to expand students' vocabulary.

2. After having the class identify the attributes of several passages, direct the students to find excellent examples of show, not tell passages from their books and record them. Give them strips of paper. Their task is to record one passage on each strip and on the back of the strip to include the page numbers and feelings described.

3. Give students about 20 minutes to find as many examples as they can record. Remind them that they will need enough of the passage that others could recognize the attributes, even if they hadn't read the book.

4. In small groups, students share examples. Students try to guess the character's feelings from the passages. Have each table group discuss their findings: Which are the best examples of the Show, Don't Tell technique?
5. Glue the passages to a piece of chart paper and use for future reference. As a homework assignment, have students look for and record great Show, Don't Tell passages that they find in their home reading in a log.

Session 3: Revising

1. Ask students to select a draft in their portfolio for Show, Don't Tell revision. Direct them to find two places where their writing might be improved by revising what is obvious or turning telling into showing. They can use a highlighter to identify these areas. Teach students to use a cut-and-paste technique with cello tape, scissors and paper to insert when needed.
2. Have students reread their piece several times to ensure a logical flow of ideas. Ask them to consider, "Does your revision make sense and improve the piece by creating voice and personality? Does your revision bring the writing to life and make it more interesting? Does the revision fit the character and plot?"
3. Give the students time to draft and revise.
4. Share the writing in partners. Make showing, not telling a focus for the conferences.

> Remember the writing anchor: Show, don't tell.

Student Reflection

- During the table work, what did you notice when you read the passages of others?
- What will you remember about showing, not telling in reading a book? in your writing?
- How did you try to create personality and characterization in your writing?
- What words work really well and stand out for you in your piece?
- What did you enjoy about this lesson? in this writing?
- How might we improve this activity?

Evaluation

To what extent was the student able to
- use the Show, Don't Tell revision to bring the writing to life and improve the piece?
- revise to give a logical flow with the rest of the piece?
- fit the character with the revision?

In this short piece, a Grade 4 student effectively shows the grief felt over her grandfather's death.

In late September the funeral was held in the Sutton Place Hotel. At the funeral I saw my relatives and my family's friends. When I looked at them, their heads hung low and they were in deep despair. I didn't understand but then I realized it was for my Papa and then I did exactly as they did and hung my head low and began to weep.

Madison

The Button Jar

Why teach this anchor lesson?

- To create a character profile
- To encourage character development and detail in writing
- To create a dialogue between two characters

How to do it

Special instructions: Gather or borrow a variety of distinctive buttons enough for everyone in the class to have one.

1. Brainstorm a list of "character qualities" and categorize them as either positive or negative. (Refer to BLM 5.4.)
2. From an interesting collection of buttons in a jar or basket, pick a button and "visualize" the type of garment it was found on. Be specific and descriptive. Describe in detail the physical and personal qualities of the person who owned the garment. Ask the students to close their eyes and imagine the character as you describe him or her.
3. Next, model filling in a draft form featuring the following questions to be answered:

   - Who is this character? Man? Woman? Boy? Girl?
   - Where does this character live?
   - What sort of person is this character?
   - What is the character's family like?

   Include space for the students to make up and answer their own questions.
4. Students choose a button with eyes closed, using only their sense of touch. This simple way of proceeding prevents them from pre-selecting a certain type of button or spending too much time choosing.
5. Create the criteria for a good description of character. (You can picture the character in your mind; you know if you would like or dislike this person; vivid language is used to describe the character.)
6. Students write character profiles describing their characters, complete with sketches of their buttons. In conferences, help students edit writing with the focus on individual needs: adding more detail; combining sentences together; checking for verb endings, incomplete sentences, punctuation, and so on.
7. Author's Chair: Selected pieces are shared with the group to be appreciated and celebrated. Students also share in partners.
8. To extend the writing experience, students share again, this time putting two characters together in a particular situation: for example, at a hockey match, on a deserted island, in a doctor's waiting room. They hold a conversation in role as the two characters. Working together, students write the dialogue that takes place between their characters. As a follow-up, they can act out their dialogue for the class.

Remember the writing anchors: Play with words! Speak!

Student Reflection

- Did you make your characters as real as possible? How did you do that?
- Did you use "rich" language and descriptive words in your writing?
- Did you enjoy the button experience? Why?
- Can a reader visualize and understand your character?

Evaluation

To what extent was the student able to
– develop the character well in the profile?
– use varied language with some sensory detail?
– use appropriate and effective dialogue?

After modelling how a button can help you make a personal connection, ask students to bring a "special" button from home that helps them make personal connections. Invite them to write a short story about their personal button connections and share with the class.

My Imagination Is My Guide: Using Guided Imagery

With guided imagery

- details and descriptions are vivid
- hints of characters' moods and emotions are present
- choice of words creates a picture in the reader's mind
- stories are believable even when imaginary
- individual interpretations are unique

Imagery enhances originality!

Some books we have used for this activity include *The Snail's Spell* and *Lizard in the Sun*, both by Joanne Ryder; *Stella, Queen of the Snow* by Marie Louise Gay; *Sylvester and the Magic Pebble* and *Abel's Island*, both by William Steig .

Be prepared for the students to journey in their imaginations to unpredictable places.

Why teach this anchor lesson?

- To give students an opportunity to develop their expressive writing by assuming the role of a character
- To help students add rich, descriptive language to a story by imagining the sensory experience
- To help students add personal voice to the writing through their word choice

How to do it

1. Select a story or a passage from a novel that has powerful descriptive language. Read it to the class. Afterwards, think about the setting and the characters and take the students on an imaginary journey into that place. Have the students close their eyes and guide them to imagine that they are in the setting of the story. They are slowly changing into the character, shrinking to become a snail, sitting in the marketplace resting after a hard morning's work, playing in the snow, shipwrecked on an open raft—whatever the story suggests.

   "Who are you? What does it feel like? What are you thinking?"

   Lead the students through a sensory journey for two or three minutes.

2. Have the students turn to the person beside them and tell them what they imagined (talking out their story).
3. Ask a few students to share their ideas with the whole group.
4. Prompt a few students to share how they will begin their writing.
5. Students go off to write. Stop every 5 to 10 minutes and ask students to share what they have written so far. (It helps students who are stuck when they hear the ideas of others.)

> Remember the writing anchor: Play with words!

Student Reflection

- How did using this strategy help you write?
- Did using the five senses help you extend your writing?
- When could you use this strategy again?

Evaluation

To what extent was the student able to
– use sensory language to describe the experience?
– let his or her individual voice be heard?
– choose words with care?
– write to convey feelings and ideas?

* A SUMMERS DAY *

A little stump and a nature carved chair in a Bowen Island forest. I can smell pine as sweet as a summers day, and a scent of cold salty air hanging in the breeze. So fresh. I can see patches of light blue sky with frothy white clouds through the different types of trees. I can hear the sound of childrens' joyful laughter and the sounds of birds chirping and flying to and fro. The sound of waves breaking on the cliffs of the beach excites me. It makes me feel relaxed and care-free.

Through Different Eyes

Why teach this anchor lesson?

- To show how changing perspective can lead to an engaging story
- To learn that personal feelings, experiences and observations can help you add detail to your writing
- To encourage vivid language use

How to do it

Session 1: Observing what's around us

1. If the book is available, read *Two Bad Ants* by Chris Van Allsburg. Alternatively, discuss with the students what it would be like to be an ant in a kitchen. You can use the guided imagery technique again.
2. Discuss with the students how everyday objects would seem different when described from an ant's point of view. (For example, a cup of tea becomes a hot brown lake; grass becomes a forest; grains of sugar are crystals.)
3. Ask the students to look around the room and list what objects they see.
4. Let each student share observations with a partner. Show that everyone has a unique list.
5. Explain that the places where we live, work and play are a large part of the writer's experience. We write best about what we know best. Students will refer to their lists in writing their paragraphs or stories.
6. Have the students expand their lists by adding colors, sounds, tastes, smells and textures. They can also list their feelings about objects and places in the classroom.

Session 2: Writing as ants

1. Tell the students that they are each going to write a paragraph or story from the perspective of an ant in the classroom. Discuss possible lead sentences for this version as a class and in partners, then let students begin writing. Students having difficulty getting started may use a lead that you have generated.
2. Circulate and conference with students. Focus on using language that will be evocative of the ant's experience in the classroom. How can language be used to convey the scale?
3. Students mumble-read, then share with a partner. Partners ask a question, give a positive response and may make one suggestion.
4. The stories may be collected into a class book. The art technique used by Chris Van Allsburg — line drawing and shading, and the use of sepia tones — may be taught and used for illustrations.

> Remember the writing anchors: Make it your own! Tell details only the writer knows. Play with words!

- Did changing the perspective make the story writing interesting to you? How?
- How did making a list help you to get ready to write?
- How can you use this technique again?

Evaluation

To what extent was the student able to
– describe accurately using good detail?
– use varied language, sense, and flow in the writing?
– use detail and varied sentence structure?

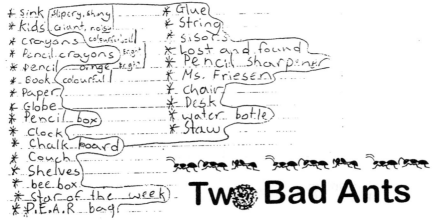

* Sink slipery, shiny
* kids giant, noisy
* crayons colourful
* Pencil crayons sharp
* Pencil orange bright
* Book colourful
* Paper
* Globe
* Pencil box
* Clock
* Chalk board
* Couch
* Shelves
* bee box
* Star of the week
* P.E.A.R bag

* Glue
* String
* sisors
* Lost and found
* Pencil sharpener
* Ms. Friesen
* chair
* Desk
* water botle
* Staw

Two Bad Ants

This Grade 3 student sample shows how adopting a different perspective makes a story set in a familiar place interesting.

The two ant's stayed behind
as the others marched right
out the door "Lets go explore,"
said one. "Yeah we could
stay here forever with out
giving our queen the good
stuff." "Hey look at that
hole" said one. "Where?"
said the other "There,
over there. Come on I'll
show you." But when they
got inside it started to
turn and spin. The ants
were scard to death.
But then it stoped.
All tiered out the ants
as quietly quickly as they could
they colwed out of the hole. Then
they heared I fimilar
sound it was their
family they quickly
going the end of the line
and safly went home.

THE END

Story Grammar 1

Name: _____   Date: _____

Story _____

Characters	Setting

Problem

Main Events	Solution

Story Grammar 2

Name: _____ Date: _____

Title: _____ Author: _____

Setting

Where? _____

_____

When? _____

_____

Characters

_____ _____

_____ _____

_____ _____

_____ _____

Problem

_____

_____

_____

_____

_____

_____

_____

_____

_____

_____

Events

_____

_____

_____

_____

_____

_____

_____

_____

_____

_____

Solution

_____

_____

_____

_____

_____

_____

_____

_____

_____

_____

Showing, Not Telling

- Henry's heart hurt and he cried for an hour.

- John and Bob jumped up and down. All the hard work the team had done had at last paid off. They were going to the championships.

- "Oh, not another broken dish!" thought Mary, as she felt a lump grow in her throat. "What will Mom say?"

- Lindsay reached the classroom door as books tumbled from her arms. She fumbled for the doorknob, knowing she was late for the field trip. Her heart sank as she looked at the empty classroom

Character Traits

Positive Character Traits	
alert	intuitive
ambitious	kind
brave	leader
capable	levelheaded
carefree	likeable
cautious	mysterious
clever	optimistic
competent	organized
conscientious	outgoing
courageous	outspoken
courteous	persuasive
creative	pleasant
curious	polite
determined	practical
easygoing	quick-thinking
friendly	resourceful
gentle	self-reliant
good friend	sensible
good worker	sensitive
happy	shrewd
happy-go-lucky	skilled
hardworking	sympathetic
helpful	thinks before acting
honest	thorough
hopeful	thoughtful
humorous	thrifty
imaginative	tireless
independent	tough
industrious	trusting

Negative Character Traits	
acts without thinking	lazy
aggressive	liar
aloof	lonely
angry	mean
belligerent	miserable
bitter	moody
boastful	nervous
boring	nuisance
bully	obstinate
clumsy	obnoxious
cold	outspoken
confused	pessimistic
cowardly	pressured by peers
crabby	quick-temoered
crafty	repulsive
cranky	rude
cruel	ruthless
dependent	sad
devious	shrewd
dishonest	shy
disorganized	sly
embarrassed easily	sneaky
foolish	snobbish
fussy	solemn
gloomy	spoiled
hateful	stubborn
helpless	stupid
hesitant	thoughtless
jealous	unfriendly

Read-Alouds to Motivate Young Authors

Aliki. *Painted Words.*

Allinson, Beverley. *Effie.*

Angelou, Maya. *Life Doesn't Frighten Me.*

Bailey, Linda, and Bill Slavin. *Adventures with the Vikings.*

Baker, Jeannie. *Where the Forest Meets the Sea.*

Barrett, Joyce Durham. *Willie's Not the Hugging Kind.*

Baylor Byrd. *Everybody Needs a Rock.*

_____. *I'm in Charge of Celebrations.*

Bloom, Becky. *Wolf.*

Booth, David. *Images of Nature: Canadian Poets and the Group of Seven.*

Bouchard, Dave. *If You're Not from the Prairie.*

Bridges, Shirin Yim. *Ruby's Wish.*

Brown, Anthony. *Voices in the Park.*

Bunting, Eve. *Fly Away Home.*

_____. *Night of the Gargoyles.*

_____. *Smoky Night.*

Cherry, Lynne. *The Great Kapok Tree.*

Clements, Andrew. *Big Al.*

Cooney, Barbara. *Miss Rumphius.*

Fitch, Sheree. *No Two Snowflakes.*

Fleischman, Paul. *Westlandia.*

Fleming, Fergus, and Karen Tomlins. *Greek Gazette.*

Friedman, Ina R. *How My Parents Learned to Eat.*

Gay, Marie-Louise. *Stella, Queen of the Snow.*

Gibbons, Gail. *The Honey Makers.*

Graham, Elspeth, and Mal Peet, compilers. *Creatures, Kings, and Scary Things.* Anthology 3.

_____. *Wolves, Eyes, and Stormy Seas.* Anthology 4.

Greenfield, Eloise. *She Come Bringing Me That Little Baby Girl.*

Heidbreder, Robert. *Don't Eat Spiders.*

Henkes. Kevin. *Chrysanthemum.*

Hoffman, Mary. *Amazing Grace.*

Hooper, Meredith. *The Pebble in My Pocket: A History of Our Earth.*

Hundal, Nancy. *I Heard My Mother Call My Name.*

Jam, Teddy. *The Stoneboat.*

Joosse, Barbara. *Mama, Do You Love Me?*

Kimmel, Eric. *Anansi and the Moss-Covered Rock.*

Laden, Nina. *The Night I Followed the Dog.*

_____. *Roberto the Insect Architect.*

Lawson, Julie. *A Morning to Polish and Keep.*

LeBox, Annette. *Salmon Creek.*

Leigh, Nila K. *Learning to Swim in Swaziland.*

Lesynski, Loris. *Dirty Dog Boogie.*

Livingstone, Myra Cohn. "Whispers."

Locker, Thomas. *Water Dance.*

London, Jonathan. *Like Butter on Pancakes.*

_____. *The Condor's Egg.*

Macdonald, Fiona, and Mark Bergin. *Inca Town.*

Mazer, Anne. *The Yellow Button.*

McGugan, Jim. *Josepha: A Prairie Boy's Story.*

Muth, Jon. *The Three Questions.*

Nicolson, Cynthia Pratt. *Volcano.*

_____. *Earthquake.*

Nicolson, Robert. *The Maya.*

O'Neill, Mary Le Duc. *Hailstones and Halibut Bones: Adventures in Color.*

Oppenheimer, Joanne. *Have You Seen Bugs?*

Paolilli, Paul, and Dan Brewer. *Silver Seeds.*

Polacco, Patricia. *The Keeping Quilt.*

Powell, Anton, and Philip Steele. *The Greek News.*

Raven, Margot Theis. *Mercedes and the Chocolate Pilot.*

Red Sky at Night: *Weather Poems.*

Ryder, Joanne. *Lizard in the Sun.*

_____. *The Snail's Spell.*

_____. *Where Butterflies Grow.*

Scieszka, Jon. *The True Story of the Three Little Pigs.*

Sendak. Maurice. *Where the Wild Things Are.*

Swope, Sam. *The Araboolies of Liberty Street.*

Tan, Shaun. *The Red Tree.*

Tanaka, Shelley. *Secrets of the Mummies: Uncovering the Bodies of Ancient Egyptians.*

Tsuchiya, Yukio. *Faithful Elephants.*

Van Allsburg, Chris. *The Mysteries of Harris Burdick.*

_____. *The Stranger.*

_____. *Two Bad Ants.*

_____. *The Widow's Broom.*

Viorst, Judith. *Alexander and the Terrible, Horrible, No Good, Very Bad Day.*

Weiss, George David, and Bob Thiele. *What a Wonderful World.*

Wells, Rosemary. *Yuko's Paper Cranes.*

Wiesner, David. *Tuesday.*

Wild, Margaret. *Fox.*

Wright, Kit. "The Magic Box."

Yee, Paul. *Roses Sing on New Snow.*

Yin. *Coolies.*

Yolen, Jane. *All Those Secrets of the World.*

_____. *Owl Moon.*

Zolotow, Charlotte. *The Seashore Book.*

Professional Bibliography

Applebee, Arthur. 1978. *The Child's Concept of Story*. Chicago: University of Chicago Press.

Atwell, Nancie. 1998. *In the Middle: New Understandings About Writing, Reading, and Learning*. Portsmouth, NH: Heinemann.

Bettleheim, Bruno. 1976. *The Uses of Enchantment*. New York: Knopf.

Calkins, Lucy McCormick. 1994. *The Art of Teaching Writing*. Portsmouth, NH: Heinemann.

Calkins, Lucy McCormick, and Shelley Harwayne. 1991. *Living Between the Lines*. Toronto: Irwin Publishing.

Chapman, Marilyn L. 1997. *Weaving Webs of Meaning: Writing in the Elementary School*. Toronto: ITP Nelson.

Egan, Kieran. 1988. *Primary Understanding: Education in Early Childhood*. New York: Routledge.

Fletcher, Ralph. 1993. *What a Writer Needs*. Portsmouth, NH: Heinemann.

Fletcher, Ralph, and JoAnn Portalupi. 2001. *Writing Workshop: The Essential Guide*. Portsmouth, NH: Heinemann.

Graves, Donald. 1983. *Writing: Teachers and Children at Work*. Portsmouth, NH: Heinemann.

Harste, Jerome C., Kathy Short, and Carolyn Burke. 1988. *Creating Classrooms for Authors: The Reading–Writing Connection*. Portsmouth, NH: Heinemann.

Harley, Avis. 2001. *Leap into Poetry: An ABC of Poetry*. Wordsong/Boyds Mills.

_____. 2001. *Leap into Poetry: More ABCs of Poetry*. Wordsong/Boyds Mills.

Harvey, Stephanie. 1998. *Nonfiction Matters: Reading, Writing, and Research in Grades 3–8*. Portland, ME: Stenhouse.

Harwayne, Shelley. 1992. *Lasting Impressions: Weaving Literature into the Writing Workshop*. Portsmouth, NH: Heinemann.

Moffett, James. 1968. *Teaching the Universe of Discourse*. New York: Houghton.

Murray, Donald. 1989. *Expecting the Unexpected: Teaching Myself and Others to Read and Write*.

Portalupi, JoAnn, and Ralph Fletcher. 2001. *Nonfiction Craft Lessons: Teaching Information Writing K–8*. Portland, ME: Stenhouse.

Ruef, Kerry. 1992. *The Private Eye (5X) Looking/Thinking by Analogy*. Seattle, WA: The Private Eye Project.

Routman, Regie. 1995. *Invitations: Changing as Teachers and Learners K–12*. Portsmouth, NH: Heinemann Educational Books.

_____. 2000. *Kids' Poems: Teaching First Graders to Love Writing Poetry*. New York: Scholastic.

_____. 2000. *Kids' Poems: Teaching Second Graders to Love Writing Poetry*. New York: Scholastic.

Smith, Frank. 1988. *Insult to Intelligence: The Bureaucratic Invasion of Our Classrooms*. Portsmouth, NH: Heinemann.

_____. 1982. *Writing and the Writer*. London: Heinemann.

Stead, Tony. 2002. *Is That a Fact? Teaching Non-Fiction Writing K–3.* Portland, ME: Stenhouse.

Strickland, Dorothy S., and Lesley Mandel Morrow, eds. 2000. *Beginning Reading and Writing.* Newark, NJ: International Reading Association.

Swartz, Larry. 2002. *The New Dramathemes.* 3d edition. Markham, ON: Pembroke.

Wells, Jan, and Linda Hart-Hewins. 1996. *Phonics, Too!* Markham, ON: Pembroke.

Wood Ray, Katie. 1999. *Wondrous Words.* Urbana, IL: National Council Teachers of English.

Index